GUIDE TO
AUTHENTICATING

by   Kevin Martin

"Trusted by Collectors and Dealers"

Odyssey Publications Inc.

Publisher : Odyssey Publications Inc.
Cover Design : Type F Typography
Editor : Kevin Martin
Interior Design and Layout : Andjelika Martin
Copyright 1999 Odyssey Publications Inc.

Printed in the United States of America
1999 Edition, First Printing
10 9 8 7 6 5 4 3 2 1

ISBN # 0-9669710-1-9

Library of Congress Catalog Card Number : #99-62978

Odyssey Publications Inc.
510-A So. Corona Mall
Corona, CA 91719
www.authenticationguide.com
www.AutographCollector.com

PREFACE

Although the purpose of this book is to help collectors authenticate autographed items, it should be regarded as a guideline in the broadest sense.

Just as you might read medical literature to compare remedies or symptoms while under a doctor's care, in the same way the wisest collectors will utilize the experienced autograph dealer as the final word in authentication.

Experienced dealers have handled more variants, secretarials and other autographed material than anyone else, and therefore are by far the most valuable source of information in the field. While it is not possible to condense those years of hands-on experience into one volume, I believe the information contained in this book will pay for itself many times over.

Happy Collecting!

Kevin Martin

ACKNOWLEDGMENTS

I wish to thank the following people who helped make this book a reality.

Darrell Talbert (Odyssey Publications) for his tireless effort on this and many other projects. He is a dedicated professional and there are too few of those these days.

Bill Miller (Odyssey Publications) for setting aside the time and resources needed to complete this project.

Joanne Lindsey (Odyssey Publications) for helping in the final coordination of this book.

Ev Phillips (Odyssey Publications) for taking time from his busy schedule to proof this book.

To all the fine dealers you will see listed in these pages, many of which helped in the compilation of this book, my heartfelt thanks.

Kevin Martin

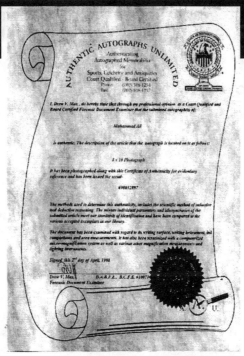

Volume 1 · 1999
$2.00

TRULY UNIQUE COLLECTIBLES

INSIDE THIS ISSUE:

- Beatles
- Buffy Vampire Slayer
- Dawson's Creek
- Elvis
- Friends
- Grateful Dead
- Jerry Garcia
- Indiana Jones
- Kiss
- John Lennon
- McGwire & Sosa
- Rolling Stones
- Scream
- Spice Girls
- Star Trek
- Star Wars Trilogy
- Titanic
- Woodstock
- X-Files
- Yankees
- And More Cool Stuff!!

Buffy Poster $10

COLLECTIBLE POP CULTURE

CALL FOR OUR NEW CATALOG FEATURING THE LARGEST SELECTION OF
AUTOGRAPHS • POSTERS • PHOTOS • TOYS • AMERICANA & MORE !!

Visit our new & improved Website to view or purchase over 10,000 products on-line at **WWW.UNIQUECOLLECTIBLES.COM**
The website is updated daily with new products & information.

Truly Unique Collectibles
MOVIES • TV • MUSIC • SCI-FI • SPORTS • MODELS

FOR ORDERS, INFORMATION OR TO RECEIVE A FREE COLOR CATALOG
CALL US TOLL FREE AT 1-888-725-7614
VISIT OUR SALES GALLERY AT - 85 MAIN STREET, NYACK, NEW YORK 10960

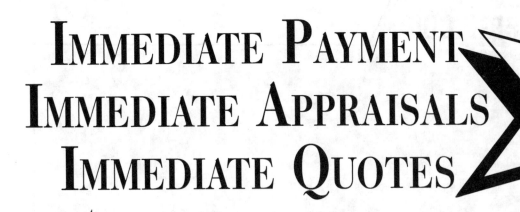

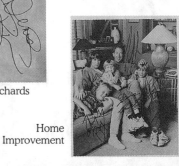

TABLE OF CONTENTS

How Do You Authenticate An Autograph?

There are many ways collectors can and should learn to authenticate the autographed pieces in their collections. While there are times you should rely on experts to authenticate for you, it adds to the fun and excitement of the hobby – not to mention your own comfort – to be able to make your own judgement as to whether or not an autograph is genuine. If you are considering purchasing an autograph, deal only with recognized experts.

Because this edition deals exclusively with entertainment autographs, we will concentrate on authenticating photographs and signatures. To that end, we'll cover such topics as pens and their respective inks, pencil, photographic stock, printed signatures, rubber stamps, secretarials and autopened signatures.

Pens/Ink and Pencil

Entertainment collectors will encounter three types of pens and ink. Knowing which one you are looking at may allow you to spot a forgery without any further research!

It will be helpful for you to memorize the era in which each pen was developed. That way, if you know when the entertainer whose signature you are examining passed away, you have two pieces of information to help you authenticate it. If the entertainer is still alive, try to find out when he or she signed the piece.

For example, Will Rogers, the famous folk comedian/actor, died in a plane crash in the 1930s long before ballpoint pens were in use. Bela Lugosi of Dracula fame died in the late 1950s, long before the Sharpie or any other marker-style pen came into existence. If you encounter a ballpoint pen signature of Rogers, or a Lugosi photograph signed with a Sharpie, both would be forgeries based on the fact that these items were not available to them during their lifetimes.

You may think forgers wouldn't make such stupid mistakes, but many don't do their homework before they forge. Recently we were asked to authenticate a signed Princess Diana magazine photograph. But upon removing it from its frame, we discovered that on the back of the signed magazine page was a tribute article published after her death!

Not all forgers are bright!

FOUNTAIN PENS are the oldest form of ink writing instruments that entertainment collectors encounter.

During Hollywood's heyday following the advent of talking motion pictures in the 1920s and '30s, fountain pens were used exclusively not only in Tinseltown, but elsewhere as well. In most cases, fountain pen ink from this earlier time period fades. However, certain black India inks are known to stay quite dark and sharp even decades later.

Under a magnifying glass you should be able to see nib tracks on most fountain pen signatures. These are the tiny indentations in the paper made by the metal tip or "nib" of the fountain pen as the signature is made, although not all fountain pens leave noticeable tracks. Pilot rollerball pens of the 1980s and today, as well as other more modern fountain pens, do not leave this pattern. However, many fountain pens that have the old-fashioned metal tips are still being used today, so these are guidelines for research only.

Do not be thrown by wild-colored inks from the '20s and '30s. Inks of purple, red, aqua, blue, black and other colors were available during those years.

Cheaper black inks of the period often oxidized with the passage of time, leaving the signature a brown color. This is typically encountered in collecting signatures from that era.

BALLPOINT PENS

The earliest ballpoint pens had an experimental ink that was an oil-based dye solution that dried slowly, causing skipping and blotting. As a result, signatures smeared easily. They also faded terribly. It wasn't until 1954 that the ink was improved, and ballpoint pens became more reliable. With this breakthrough, ballpoint pens soared in popularity.

Fine Point Markers

Like the "Magic Marker" brands, these markers faded terribly after only a few days exposure to light. Black ink often leaves a yellowish halo effect around the signature as well. These were introduced in a variety of colors around 1964.

THE SHARPIE IS BORN

About the same time (1963), the Sanford company introduced the "Sharpie" pen. Sharpies hit the market in only one color – black. The point was much wider than the other markers, but it wrote on virtually any surface and dried quickly and permanently. In late 1964 Sanford introduced blue ink. But the company struggled, and Sharpies didn't come into widespread use until the late 1970s. In fact, Sharpie signatures are rarely encountered prior to that time.

Metallic gold and silver pens date from this same period (1978 to present).

TIP: A Sharpie works almost like paint. Forgers use this to their advantage by erasing, retracing and blending lines together – all features that would not be present in an authentic signature. How can you tell? The answer is simple. Using a magnifying glass, see if the width or thickness of the lines varies. If it does, it means the pen has been through the area more than once. A small difference is hard to spot with the naked eye, but is more noticeable when viewed through a magnifier.

Also look for signs of erasing. You should almost hope to find traces of a removed inscription – at least then you know someone was trying to make an authentic signature more valuable. Ironically, removing an inscription is one time the forger helps you out. Of course, if you see that the name itself has been erased and rewritten, it is likely that you have a forgery on your hands.

Starts and stops in signatures, or faltering of any kind, are all clues to detecting forgeries. These tell-tale signs are easier to see under magnification.

Do not be impressed by dealers who have photographs of themselves and celebrities even if the star is signing in the shot. This is no more proof of authenticity than a person telling you a story about how they acquired the signature. Rely on comparison to known authentic examples and dealers with the expertise to authenticate - not on stories and pictures!

Before we go into this portion of the authentication process, it will help if you understand a few simple terms we will use in studying signatures.

A BASELINE is an imaginary line on which a signature seems to rest.

An ASCENDER is the part of a letter or name that extends above the rest of the signature body. A DESCENDER is that part (if any) that extends below the baseline of the signature.

HEIGHT and WIDTH of a signature refers to the size up and down and left to right of a person's signature. These usually don't vary except in cases where a person deliberately wants to sign an item larger or smaller due to space limitations.

A SIGNATURE BREAK refers to the space between names in a signature or spaces within the name where one pen stroke ends and a new one begins. These are usually very consistent in most signatures.

SLANT refers to the degree and direction a signature leans.

What if a dealer tells you the reason the signature they are selling you looks a little different because the signature was "rushed?"

Rushed Signatures

Much has been written about the "rushed" signature (as when the star signs while crossing the street) as opposed to the "They were sitting down or taking their time" signature. Are there differences between the two? There is, of course, but here is where handwriting analysis comes in handy.

Try this yourself: Take a full-size sheet of paper and start signing at the top as slowly and as neatly as you can. Then sign again and again, faster and faster and faster down the page, gaining speed each time.

You will see that when a signature is in fact "rushed," the only thing that happens is that certain letters become less formed or disappear entirely. BUT – and this is a very important BUT – the characteristics, i.e. slant, style, etc. remain consistent. In other words, you don't begin to spell differently, change the overall height and width of your letter formation, capitalize things you usually lowercase and vice versa. So no matter what the provenance or story behind a piece, remember this motto: "An autograph either IS or IS NOT authentic based on its own merits!"

One final word on buying "rushed," "variations," and other flawed autograhs ... you will be much happier in the long run by being patient and waiting for a nice clean typical example to be offered to you and you won't have to constantly explain its flaws to other people. Let someone else collect the taped, stained, smeared, rushed and other fixer-uppers while you build a world class collection.

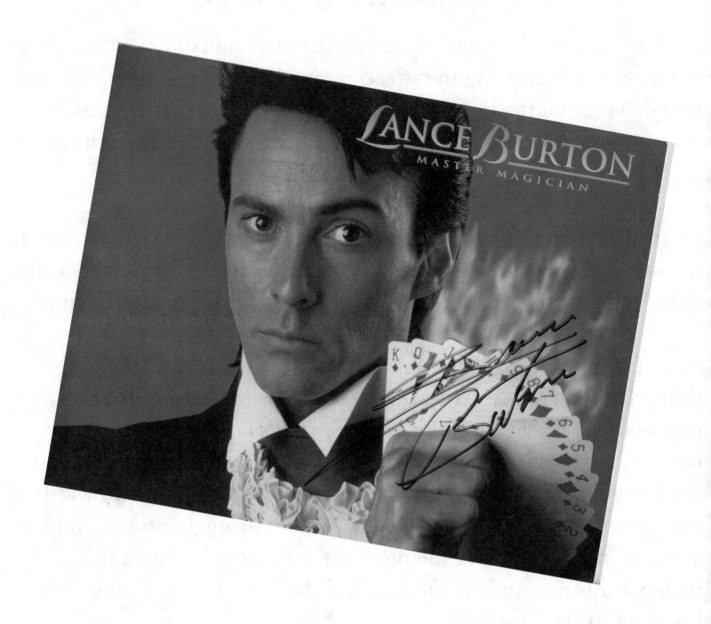

The author got this program of master magician Lance Burton signed "In Person" after one of his shows in Las Vegas. However, Burton has been known to sign fan mail as well. Signed by mail or in person, the value would be the same. The "In Person" element is more fun for the fan, of course, and may be the only way to obtain signatures from stars who do not sign their mail.

I Got It In-Person

In-Person. Here's a term that is abused more than a buffet by Luciano Pavarotti.

Dealers often use the term "In-Person" when advertising signed pieces in their stock. The term was first coined in the early 1980s when a small but dedicated group of autograph hounds realized they could sell the extra photographs they got signed while chasing celebrities. Some even made a living out of doing this on a full-time basis. They developed an intricate network of paid "helpers" who tipped them off about when and where stars were scheduled to be, and became adept at cornering them, sometimes several times in a day. Often employing friends to increase their odds and boost the numbers of signed photographs, many of them enjoyed great success.

On the surface, this seemed to be a good thing. After all, these autograph hounds provided a much-needed service to collectors who, for a variety of reasons, didn't have such access and couldn't obtain signed items from certain stars through the mail.

In any human endeavor where money is involved, the greed factor eventually will play a part. Dealers have overhead in the form of rent, employees, and so on, and necessarily have to mark an item up in price to stay profitable. Let's say a dealer feels the market will pay $50 for a Jerry Seinfeld signed photo, and has to offer $25-$30 to the guy on the street – his "In-Person" source – to get one. What happened in the past was that many of these sources decided to become dealers themselves. After all, they reasoned, they were doing all the work and, after standing around airports or jogging through traffic all day, felt they should get ALL of the $50, not just the wholesale amount.

While it was true they had NO authentication experience, they dealt only in pieces they saw signed themselves – hence the term "In-Person." They began running the term "In-Person" in their catalogs and ads – with the strong implication that if you bought something that wasn't "In-Person" it may not be authentic.

Many dealers countered by running "In-Person" material in their

... They all come to us for the best in genuine in-person comtemporary autographs. Why not buy from the source?

ads and catalogs, even though they bought it from "In-Person"collectors or "dealers" and therefore had not actually seen it signed. But even *those* sources often buy second-hand, and they didn't see the material signed either, which effectively negates the term for their use as well.

In a more perfect world, wheeling and dealing like this would be our only problem. But in our not-so-perfect world we also have forg

Genuine In-Person Signed Photos

100% IN-PERSON AUTOGRAPHS

eries to worry about, and these pose an even bigger threat to collectors.

Today many stars' signatures are quite abbreviated, and are easily imitated by an accomplished artist/forger. The forger may have obtained a star's signature in person, but then copies it onto other photographs. While there are dealers and others who sell forged items, the problem certainly has become more prevalent with modern "In-Person" material.

To top it all off, many mainstream dealers who never met a celebrity in their lives began selling "In-Person" photographs and labeling them as such. But, like a distant cousin, they were at BEST once removed from the process, having bought the piece from the person who claimed to have obtained it.

He's the one everyone in Hollywood has proclaimed paparazzi with a pen.

In response to a confused marketplace, some dealers started telling their customers they employed the only "real" In-Person collectors on the street. Some even supplied the dates the pieces were signed, or pictures of the stars signing. Common sense dictates that just because you have a picture of a star signing something – indeed even signing something that *looks* like the object or photo in question – does NOT mean the item you now possess was the same one in the photograph.

I know of several cases where "In-Person" dealers have purchased what they call "photo ops" or candid pictures of a celebrity signing in a crowd from paparazzi and even other dealers. Why? Draw your own conclusion. Making the situation worse is the fact that in many signing sessions some stars will not allow their pictures to be taken if they don't like their appearance that day, or because they are afraid you might sell the photograph, or any number of legitimate reasons.

If all of this sounds grim and you get the impression that nothing out there is authentic, ~~continues to be your only place for authentic in-person autographs.~~ try to remember the motto mentioned earlier: An autograph either IS or IS NOT authentic based on its own merits, NOT on the story surrounding its birth.

Years ago the stamp collecting hobby was shocked to learn that a factory in Germany was re-gumming the backs of stamps to make them appear to be in mint condition when in fact they were not. In the poster business, a foreign factory has been cranking out "authentic" turn-of-the-century pieces. Coin collecting has been plagued from day one – as has the sports card collecting hobby – by reprints, bad grading and restorations!

Just a few years ago, even the prestigious Louvre museum in Paris had to declare that 24 Rembrandt pencil sketches it owned were forgeries – pieces people had paid money to see for dozens of years – and they maintain a staff of art experts!

Forgeries are not new to our hobby, nor is it new to many other hobbies. Yet those hobbies flourish to this day, and so does auto-graph collecting. Why? Because serious collectors learn which dealers have experience in this business, belong to reputable autograph organizations, and provide them with a place to go should they encounter any problems.

"Good Advice," you admit. But the dealer said his piece has a GREAT story behind it. The certificate of authenticity says it's "from the collection of Mr. Hornblower," or "purchased from the director of the picture," or "signed at 5th and Vine in L.A. at precisely 4 p.m. on Saturday the third of January, 1998." Proof of authenticity? Hardly.

AN AUTOGRAPH IS OR IS NOT AUTHENTIC BASED ON ITS OWN MERITS!

If careful study proves an autograph to be authentic, then and ONLY then does a story like where or when it was signed add a little fun (or value) to the piece.

But a story itself does NOT authenticate an autograph.

For decades obtaining an autograph "In-Person" was really the only way to guarantee authenticity. But this does NOT mean you should check your brain at the door and rely on the "In-Person" pledge. You still need to ask the right questions and learn how to authenticate for yourself.

Learning the authentication part of this hobby is half the fun.

Think about this: Even if the person from whom you buy a piece actually saw it signed, years later when you need to sell it, you cannot legally say that *you* saw it signed.

Who among us has seen Abraham Lincoln sign anything? OK, maybe Zsa Zsa Gabor, but surely no one else! Authentication is the ONLY reliable way to prove what you own is real.

If it doesn't look authentic, is it a forgery ?

It could be an autopen, a secretarial, a printed signature or rubber-stamped or it could be a fake. Let's examine each one.

The term "autopen" strikes terror in the hearts of collectors everywhere. But in reality an autopen is fairly easy to distinguish IF you have a good file of known autopen examples.

Autopens are mechanical devices that can sign as many as 800 identical pieces an hour for people who have large volumes of mail to sign. The first people to employ them were politicians (mayors, governors, senators, and so on), Supreme Court justices, astronauts and presidents. Today the availability and lower cost of these machines plus their ease of operation have encouraged all types of celebrities to purchase and use them.

The key to determining if your signature was made by an autopen machine is whether or not the signatures match each other EXACTLY. Not almost, not 99 percent, but PERFECT matches. No human can sign exactly the same way twice. While that sounds easy to do, try it and you'll find that no matter how consistent your signing habits, you cannot sign the same way twice. Your signature is like a snowflake in this regard.

But an autopen signs EXACTLY the same way EVERY TIME IT SIGNS. This is because it follows a plastic pattern made from an signature example you provide in advance. The plastic template is inserted in the machine and off it goes!

The easiest way to identify a signature as an autopen is to superimpose the suspect example on a known autopen example. If possible, copy the signatures onto clear Mylar film for this purpose. Otherwise, check two signatures side by side. First check the length of the signatures. If they are exact, then check the height and so on. If ANY element of the signature in question does not match the known autopen example, then yours is NOT an autopen.

Today autopens can trace short sentences such as "Best Wishes," and can insidiously shift between salutations and signatures. For example, the machine can sign "Best Wishes" in the top left of a photograph and sign the celebrity's name in the lower right.

Autopen machines can use any pen, pencil or Sharpie that is put into its little mechanical hand, so the ink that is used has no bearing on authenticity.

The tricky part comes when someone who uses an autopen makes up a new plastic "matrix" for the machine at a later date. Remember, no human signs EXACTLY the same way twice, so when a new matrix is needed down the road (they do wear out), a new example of the celebrity's signature is submitted, and a new, slightly different matrix is made.

Research is critical when trying to nail down autopen usage. Whenever a collector/dealer or researcher finds two signatures that are EXACT, a clean copy of one should be made and circulated as an autopen example. Some people like Richard Nixon have had as many as 20 different autopen examples made during their careers including first names and, in Nixon's case, one made to sign his initials!

As of this writing, we know of newer autopen models that also can sign non-flat items such as baseballs! Be careful, and learn all you can about known autopen patterns for given celebrities.

See the Appendix for a list of publications that are known to publish autopen patterns, and for some additional suggested reading on this subject.

KNOWN AUTOPENS

The following celebrities have been known to use autopens.

Jimmy Stewart
Paul Newman
Joe Pesci
Robert Duval
Elizabeth Shue

PRINTED SIGNATURES

As discussed earlier, printed signatures are fairly easy to spot by looking at the item in question in a strong light and, if possible, with a magnifier.

Unlike the marks that are raised on the back of an item when it is signed by a person, a printed signature will leave no indentation marks on the back of the paper or photograph. In addition, the ink will lack any contrast when the signature is tilted from side to side. When a printed signature is magnified, you will plainly see that it is flat and appears not to be on top of the paper fibers but, rather, underneath.

Printing in the Negative

This is a clever new process that can easily fool the viewer. Here's how it works. The celebrity takes a real 8x10 photograph and signs it, then takes a professional picture and negative of the item, and has quantities of it printed. Adding to the illusion, secretaries often will write "Best Wishes" or inscribe the photograph to the person requesting it, writing their words above the printed signature or even in another part of the photograph.

Here are some tips that will help. The illusion of printing in the negative isn't as deceptive unless the celebrity uses black ink on a black and white photograph. This is the most economical way for the star to have it printed, since color photography is far more expensive to produce.

If you are in doubt, a magnifying glass will show instantly that the signature is part of the photograph. That's because the surface will be smooth and glossy under magnification, and the signature actually appears beneath the surface. A real signature will appear to be on top of the photograph in question.

Jim Carrey wrote "Spank You Very Much!" and signed his b/w portrait, from which he had photographs printed. Now many other stars are employing this method. When looking to buy a piece, be sure to have your trusty magnifier with you, or at least remove the photograph in question from any frame or plastic sleeve. Eyeball it up close in adequate lighting, because the more space between you and the photograph, such as glass or a plastic sleeve, the more likely you are to be deceived by the illusion of authenticity.

The following is a list of celebrities who frequently send printed signatures.

Kim Alexis - 6x7 color photo

Chad Allen - 5x7 b/w photo

Woody Allen - 8x10 b/w photo

Lonnie Anderson- 8x10 color photo

Richard Dean Anderson - 4x6 color "Stargate" photo

Tom Arnold -5x7 color photo

Dan Aykroyd - 8x10 b/w with secretarial inscriptions

Kevin Bacon - 5x7 b/w photo

Tyra Banks -5x7 b/w photo

Pat Benetar - postcard

Jodi Benson - 4x6 b/w photo

Halle Berry - 4x6 color photo

Josie Bissett - 4x6 color photo

Jimmy Buffett - 8x10 b/w photo with secretarial inscriptions

Brett Butler - 5x7 b/w photo

James Caan - 8x10 b/w photo

Dick Clark - color postcard printed

Alabama - color 8x10 photo

Courteney Cox - 8x10 b/w photo

Cindy Crawford - 8x10 several different photographs

Lesley Anne Down - several different 8x10 b/w photos

Roma Downey- several different photographs - all printed

Christine Ebersole - 8x10 b/w with secretarial inscriptions

Barbara Eden - 5x7 b/w photo

Chris Farley - printed in silver

Jamie Farr - 8x10 b/w photo

Terry Farrell - 5x7 b/w photo

Calista Flockhart - 8x10 color and b/w with secretarial
inscriptions

Anne Francis - 4x5 b/w photo

Jeff Goldblum - 5x7 b/w photo

Salma Hayek - 5x7 b/w photo

Hugh Hefner - 8x10 color photo

Julio Iglesias - 8x10 b/w photo - He got fancy, printing
"Love, Julio" and "Crazy for you, Love Julio"

"Jag" cast - all four printed on b/w 8x10

Chuck Jones - printed sketches and signatures

Jenny Jones - 8x10 b/w printed

Tom Jones - 5x7 color photo

Ashley Judd - 8x10 color printed with sneaky secretarial descriptions

Lisa Kudrow- secretarial 8x10 b/w

Christine Lahti - 5x7 b/w or color postcard

Nathan Lane - 4x6 b/w photo

Lori Loughlin - color postcard

"Mad About You" cast - 8x10 b/w photo

Cheech Marin - 5x7 color photo

Jenny McCarthy - 8x10 b/w printed

Mathew McConaughey - 8x10 b/w in gold ink

"Nanny" cast - printed photo

Rene O'Connor - 8x10 color photo

Frank Oz - 8x10 b/w photo

Della Reese - 8x10 b/w photo

Christina Ricci - 4x6 b/w photo

Roseanne - 5x7 b/w photo

Adam Sandler - 4x6 b/w photo

Steven Seagal - 8x10 b/w photo

Leigh Taylor-Young - 8x10 b/w photo

Marlo Thomas - 8x10 b/w photo - printed greetings as well.

Lea Thompson - 8x10 color photo

"Touched by an Angel" - 8x10 b/w all three printed

Vince Vaughn - 5x7 b/w photo

Elija Wood - 5x7 b/w photo

James Woods - 3.5 x 5.5 b/w photo

Daphne Zuniga - 4x5 b/w photo

* We welcome collectors sending examples of other printed celebrity photographs for inclusion in future editions of this book.

Send them to:

Authentication
4521 PGA Blvd Suite 258
Palm Beach Gardens, FL 33418

All submissions become the property of Odyssey Publications, Inc.

Best wishes,

Steve Spielberg

STEVEN SPIELBERG
(PRINTED SIGNATURE)

SECRETARIALS

God bless them, these usually well-intentioned little devils have been around since time began. They are often sold on the market as real, and are encountered much more frequently than forgeries. Like a fake autograph, a secretarially-signed item is absolutely worthless. Fortunately, the vast majority of secretaries who sign entertainment autographs do NOT try to imitate with a great degree of accuracy the look of their employers' signatures. Once again, experience and a good research file will help you separate the real signatures from the fakes. However, some secretaries have been signing mail and, in some cases, even documents, for the same celebrity for decades. Along the way, they have become quite adept at imitating their bosses' signatures.

Bob Hope, Robert Redford, Paul Newman and Clint Eastwood have had secretaries in their employ for years signing their mail. All have tried to imitate their employers' signatures with varying degrees of success.

Even the handiwork of the more accomplished secretaries can be separated from authentic signatures by studying them side by side. We have published several known secretarial signatures in this book for your reference.

If you write to celebrities, keep copies of all your responses so you can compare them to examples you see offered for sale, in articles that show In-Person signatures, and on documents that come on the mar ket. By making these comparisons, you will be able to make an educated guess as to which ones are real and which are probably secretarials.

MARLON BRANDO

DREW BARRYMORE

JAMIE LEE CURTIS

WALT DISNEY

WALT DISNEY

SECRETARIAL

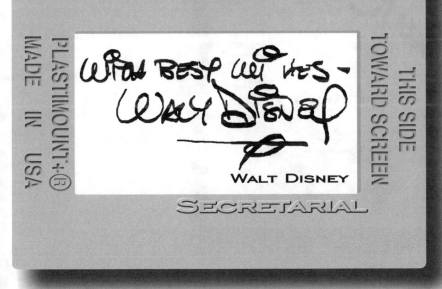

WALT DISNEY

SECRETARIAL

CLINT EASTWOOD

SECRETARIAL

Nicolas Cage

NICOLAS CAGE

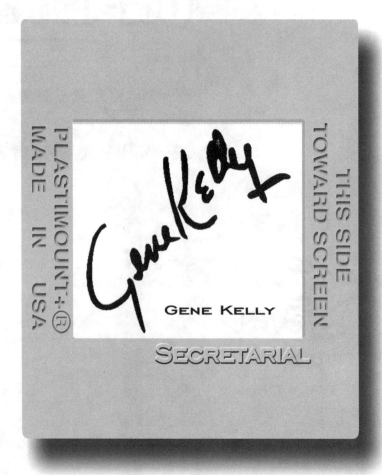

GENE KELLY

SECRETARIAL

*Paul Newman is a very tricky signature to authenticate. Be sure you are dealing with expert when adding one to your collection.

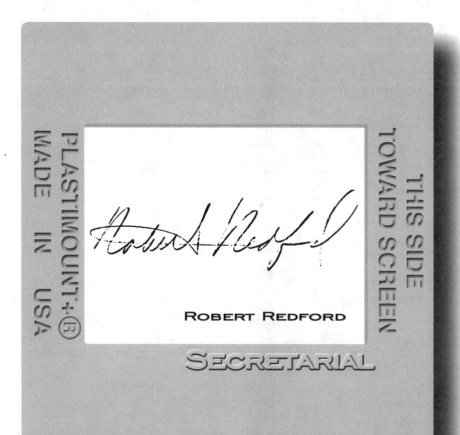

*Robert Redford sells an 8x10 authentically signed photo in his Sundance catalog for $695!!!

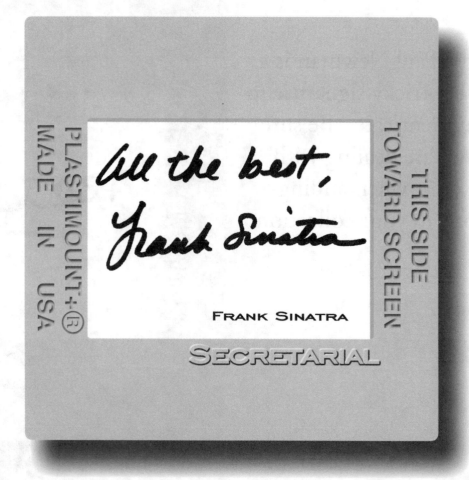

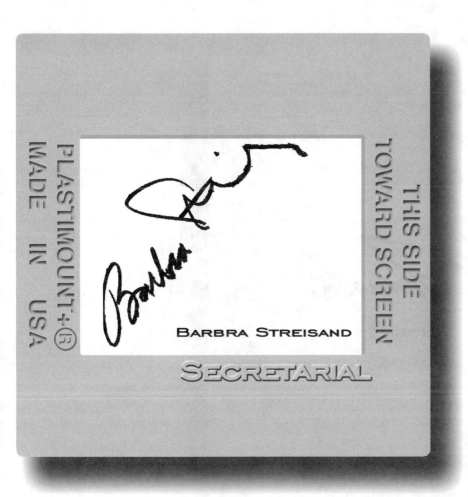

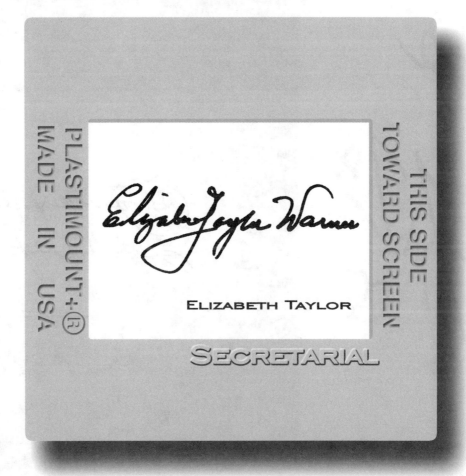

PLASTIMOUNT+® MADE IN USA

THIS SIDE TOWARD SCREEN

JOHN TRAVOLTA

SECRETARIAL

PLASTIMOUNT+® MADE IN USA

THIS SIDE TOWARD SCREEN

JOHN WAYNE

SECRETARIAL

LIZA MINELLI

RAQUEL WELCH

All my love
dear

ROBIN WILLIAMS

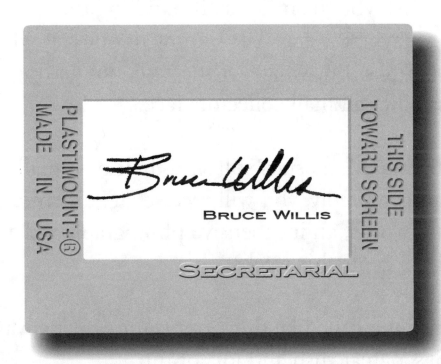

BRUCE WILLIS

GETTING RESPONSES BY MAIL

First the bad news: The vast majority of celebrity responses received through the mail are not authentic. They are either rubber stamped, printed, or signed by a secretary. Sometimes you'll get a rejection letter stating that the star cannot or will not sign or, worse still, no response at all.

There also are financial risks involved. When you send an item unsolicited, the law allows the reciepient – in this case the star – to keep it if he or she so desires.

I've heard many horror stories from collectors who had four or five signatures on a cast photo and needed just one more, only to send it out and never see it again. Maybe the office staff handling the celebrity's mail kept it or maybe the star did. I know of one star who donates such pieces to charities. But whatever the case, not getting your items back is a possibility all mail collectors face.

Now for the GOOD news. Many stars still sign their own mail. Even if it takes months to get a reply, you will receive an authentic reponse, all for a few kind words, an inexpensive photograph and a 33-cent stamp. (Is it still 33 cents this week?)

Treat writing to celebrities a little like the lottery. You won't always win, but when you do, it's a great rush and lots of fun.

Odyssey Publications will be releasing later this year a helpful book about writing to celebrities for fun and profit. It's full of tips and provides thousands of up-to-date addresses, and will be available at bookstores or by writing the publisher. See the Appendix at the back of this book for details.

Whether you collect by mail or buy from dealers who do that exclusively (many do), you still should learn to compare the autographs you receieve with examples from documents and "In-Person" sources. Use the authentication methods explained in this book, always remembering that an autograph either is or is not authentic based on its own merit.

Even if every dealer in the country sells a particular signature, that is no guarantee it's real. For 35 years Bob Hope has employed the same secretary who, in his words, "could sign my name as well as I could." Fortunately, most stars do not teach their secretaries to duplicate their signatures, but it is important to learn what you can. Buy reference sources like this one and others in the field, and visit websites like www.autographpriceguide.com and www.UACC.com. Also get the latest copy of the *The Official Autograph Collector Price Guide* so you can keep track of what your booty is worth! (See the Appendix for more information.)

Another tip: For goodness sake, invest $5 in a little magnifying glass so you don't have to guess or go blind on those tricky printed and rubber stamp jobs.

THE BROKEN PEN AWARD

The following are celebrities who do not sign in any fashion. The good news is there are no confusing secretarials, autopens or printed signatures, but then again, there aren't many real ones either! Don't bother mailing these letters. Save yourself the 33 cents.

Sir Andrew Lloyd Webber - tells collectors he "does not sign autographs except in order to raise money for charities he is connected with"

Ron Howard - returns mail stamped "Please return to sender - we are unable to sign autographs"

Kirk Douglas - for years a generous signer, now things are returned stating he is "no longer able to fulfill the numerous requests he receives each day"

Gary Burghoff - " due to sudden increased volume of my mail I am unable to process any"

Jack Lemmon - after years as a generous signer he now returns things stating "after years of never refusing my fans, I regret to write that the requests have reached a point where I have no choice but to discontinue signing items"

BUYING AT AUCTION

The best advice here is to make sure you know how to authenticate whatever you plan to bid on, and always be sure to preview the lots that interest you BEFORE you bid.

Bargains can be found at auctions, usually on the larger lots and more run-of-the-mill items that don't generate a lot of bidder action. Auctions also are an excellent source for pieces you won't normally find in dealer inventories. This is because many dealers routinely bring rare items to market through auction houses to achieve optimum prices for their finds.

157. Ronald Reagan - A color 8x10 Signed Photograph obtained In Person by a political aide a few years ago. Sadly, Mr. Reagan's Alzheimer has gotten to the point the great man now only recognizes his wife. This will only rise in value. Est: $200 - $300

158. Ronald Reagan - Pencil signed album page taken from a 40's autograph album book. Perfect for framing. Est: $100 - $200

159. Robert Redford - A one page 1974 DS regarding a film project signed by Redford. He is actually rare in authentic material as so many secretarials are being sold on the market. Est: $75 - $150

160. Keannu Reeves - The Speed star on a personal check that is also filled out by him in addition to being boldly signed. Est: $40 - $80

161. Brad Renfro - Color 8x10 SP of the young star who is appearing in the upcoming Star Wars -Prequal. Est: $50 - $90

162. Jean Reno - A color 8x10 publicity SP in character from the film Mission Impossible. Est: $40 - $80

163. Anne Rice - The Queen of horror has signed these three personal bookplates that picture her New Orleans home. Est: $50 - $100

164. Michael Richards - Color comical 8x10 SP of Kramer from Seinfeld. Est: $50 - $90

165. Michael Richards - A one page DS to star in "Young Doctors in Love" long before he would be Kramer on Seinfeld's hit TV series. Est: $50 - $100

166. Lee Ann Rimes - The cute country superstar many compare to the legendary Patsy Cline signed with her usual "LeeAnn" on a cute color 8x10 SP. Est: $40 - $75

167. Julia Roberts - Her own personal bank card for a checking account early in her acting career. Would frame nicely. The ONLY safe way to collect an actress whose authentic material is so rare. Est: $150 - $300

Know what you are looking at. Preview an auction in advance and attend in person if at all possible. Find out what the auction company's return policy is and what protection the house offers you. Then decide in advance how much you are willing to bid on an item, and STICK to that level. Auction houses count on whipping a crowd into a bidding frenzy, and then hope the bidders abandon all reason. "MUST GET LOT," you think as your eyes glaze over. If you are a competitive person, try to let sanity prevail and just have fun. Remember, there will always be another auction!

In previewing auctions, you may be surprised to find a few secretarials or outright forgeries. It has been known to happen even at the best of auction houses, especially those that sell cars one week, wine the next and then autographs, rather than specialize in autographs only. An even more important reason for previewing auctions is because the catalogs sometimes don't describe condition, flaws, smears, etc. adequately enough. Once an item is purchased, these factors aren't usually valid excuses to return it. So be careful!

BUYING FROM DEALERS/CATALOGS

The key here is to get as many different catalogs in your area of collecting interest as possible mailed to you. That way you can get a feel for the price range the items you would like to obtain. Look through each catalog as soon as you receive it, and CALL EARLY, since many items sell quickly. If a particular item has sold, ask the dealer politely if you can placed be on a waiting list in case the person who beat you to the punch doesn't come through with

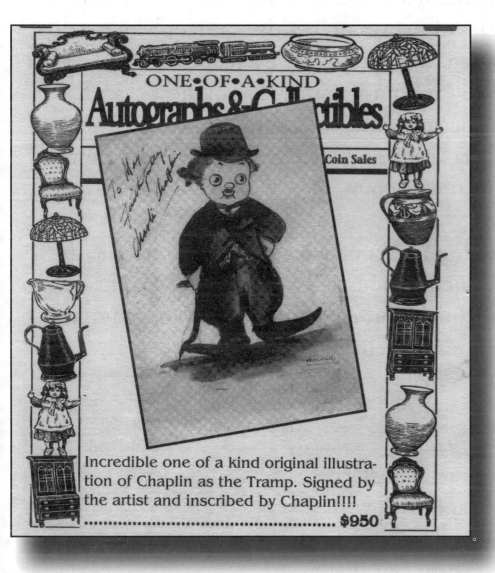

ONE·OF·A·KIND
Autographs & Collectibles
Coin Sales

Incredible one of a kind original illustration of Chaplin as the Tramp. Signed by the artist and inscribed by Chaplin!!!!
.... $950

payment. It happens all the time, and most dealers will take your name. Who knows? If it's meant to be, you may get a call and still get the piece you want.

Check each dealer's credentials. The tougher it is for him or her to qualify for membership in the ABA, IADA, PADA and the UACC dealers group, the better. All are preferable to any club that requires only the payment of dues to join. Check the Better Business Bureau in their respective cities and states to make sure they have no unresolved complaints. But DON'T fall into the trap of asking a lot of other dealers about a particular dealer OR his inventory. Like most hobbies, ours is made up of many competitive human beings, and those of us in it are flawed. Many of us have a tendency to take a shot at a fellow dealer for one reason or another that in most cases has nothing to do with the person's integrity or the authenticity of a piece. Asking other dealers is like asking K-Mart what they think of Wal-Mart. Your information is going to be a bit biased!

Instead, ask other collectors about a dealer, or ask the dealer for references. Just as with auction houses, ask the dealer what his return policy is and what authenticity protection he offers. For example, what are acceptable reasons for returning an item? Does the dealer offer a certificate of authenticity?

It is best to cultivate a relationship with only a few dealers, and stick with them as you build your collection. More may be the merrier at a party, but that's not necessarily true when it comes to collecting authentic autographs.

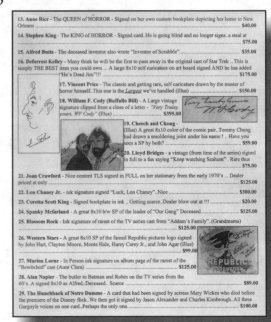

BUYING ONLINE

This may be the wave of the future, but for now it is fraught with forgeries and fly-by-night businesses.

BE CAREFUL ON THE NET – it just might not catch you when you fall! Or you may just get run over on the information highway! OK, enough jokes. But seriously folks, the best way to enjoy the Internet is to use it as a tool of convenience when contacting people with whom you ALREADY have established a relationship.

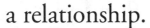

For example, you shop at Barnes and Noble bookstores. You buy from them, you like them, and now you need a title in a hurry because the local store doesn't have it in stock. You go online in the comfort of your own living room and order it from

Barnes and Noble. (If you're lounging around in your underwear, please put something on if I drop in, OK?)

But why go online and order from WESELLBOOKS.com, which has no corporate face, no track record, and no employees you can call on the phone. They may be able to supply you as well as, or even better than, Barnes and Noble. Or maybe they can't – or you just kissed your money goodbye when you gave them your credit card number!

Like anything else, if you insist on using an online service that doesn't exist in any other form, be sure you speak with several satisfied customers – preferably friends of yours who have had satisfactory experiences with the company in question. This should not be confused with testimonials on WESELLBOOKS.com posted by "Gofer46" in Maryland. Who the heck is that ? How do you reach Gofer46 to confirm that he or she was in fact treated well? How do you know Gofer46 isn't really WESELLBOOKS.com?

You see the problem here. But, if nothing else, you can peruse autograph dealers' stock online to see what they are asking for different items and, in general, educate yourself further. After all, education – not commerce – is what the Internet was founded on. So don't be in a hurry to buy solely on the Internet. Remember, there is no Better Business Bureau, mail fraud laws or any other protection out there, at least not yet. As online commerce grows, I'm sure these things will improve. But for now, be careful who you deal with and what you tell them about yourself and your collecting habits.

Autograph show tips

Tip #1 - If celebrities are signing at the show you are attending, be sure to bring your favorite pens for them to sign with rather than to rely on what they have. Sharpie brand markers are the autograph hounds' choice for many reasons. They dry VERY fast and permanently, lessening any chance of smearing, and they come in a variety of bright fade-resistant colors.

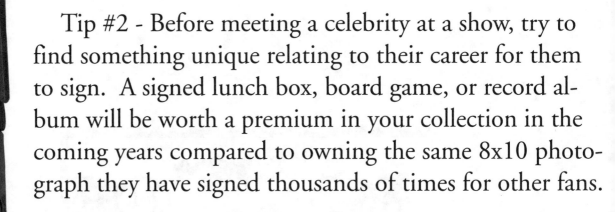

Tip #2 - Before meeting a celebrity at a show, try to find something unique relating to their career for them to sign. A signed lunch box, board game, or record album will be worth a premium in your collection in the coming years compared to owning the same 8x10 photograph they have signed thousands of times for other fans.

If you do not have any memorabilia to offer the star to sign, then ask them to draw a sketch or add a quote to the photograph to make your piece more unique.

And for the entertainment of the dealers, you could have a body part signed, a stunt made famous on the Howard Stern Show.

BUYING AT AUTOGRAPH SHOWS

Don't pass up an opportunity to attend an autograph show when one comes within driving distance of your home town. If it's farther away, try to fit it into an upcoming vacation. But, like all other forms of buying (auction houses, dealers, stores, etc.) be sure you know who you are dealing with. Ask other dealers in the room if a dealer you don't recognize is known to them. (Ask more than one dealer for his opinion so you get a fair representation. You might just pick one who is mad at him, or maybe jealous.)

Shows are social in nature, which makes them a lot of fun for collectors. So, by all means, try to get to one!

The best shows in the field are currently being run by the nations' top two autograph clubs, the IACC/DA and the UACC. The UACC states that they employ a "proctor" to deal with any collector complaints should they arise at one of their shows. The IACC/DA only allows dealers with no complaints against them and who are members of the dealers alliance to set up at their shows.

You can get a current listing of upcoming IACC/DA shows by writing their headquarters (listed under Organizations on page 69.) You can obtain a UACC show schedule by writing them as well. (see page 71)

"I don't want to belong to any club that would have me as a member."

- Groucho Marx

ORGANIZATIONS

IACC/IADA

The International Autograph Collectors Club (IACC) and Dealers Alliance (IADA) is a club for collectors and dealers established in 1997 by a group of professionals who were aware of the hobby's problems and were eager and committed to solving them.

The club is a nonprofit organization whose primary purpose is to educate the autograph community around the world and especially to ensure all collectors that they will be dealing with other IADA members who stand out amongst the rest in credentials, adhering to the industry's strongest code of ethics.

The club is dedicated in focus to only the field of autograph collecting.

The club issues six magazines per year titled *"Eyes and Ears of the Hobby"* as well as various signature studies that are invaluable reference works for collectors and dealers alike.

All members also receive a copy of the yearly Directory that is recognized as the autograph collectors safeguard.

Not every dealer who sells autographs may become an IADA member. Dealers requesting membership must be sponsored by an existing member with two references, which are thoroughly checked before membership is allowed.

Every IADA dealer must offer customers a Lifetime Guarantee Certificate of Authenticity with every item they sell.

Most importantly, the IACA/IADA assures each member that

should there arise an ethics complaint against any member, that complaint will be acknowledged and acted upon by the club's officers and board.

The club is also the only one in existence today with a physical headquarters that all members are welcome to visit.

Educational courses are offered for collectors and dealers free of charge in conjunction with the clubs autograph shows held around the country each year.

All members have access to a large autograph reference library to aid in determining authenticity.

Interested parties can learn more or request membership in the organization by writing :

IACC/IADA Headquarters

4575 Sheridan St. Suite #111

Hollywood, Florida 33021

(561) 736-8409

Fax (561) 736-5902

UACC

The Universal Autograph Collector Club is currently the largest organization for autograph collectors in the United States with over 2,000 members.

Founded in New York in 1965, the UACC is a non-profit organization whose purpose is to educate its members and the public at large about all aspects of autograph collecting through its shows, seminars and publications.

By joining the UACC you will receive the 64 page bimonthly publication called the *"Pen and Quill"* which features articles on autographs in all areas.

All members are required to adhere to a code of ethics.

UACC
Dept PG
P.O. Box 6181
Washington, DC 20044

The Professional Autograph Dealers Association ™

The name pretty much says it all. The dealers that we have encountered from this organization are experienced, knowledgeable, dedicated to customer service, and committed to a strict code of ethics. The only drawback is that the dealers mainly specialize in historical items.

For a free brochure and membership directory, write to:

Professional Autograph Dealers Association
P.O. Box 1729-A, Murray Hill Station
New York, NY 10156

The Manuscript Society

The Manuscript Society is an international society whose members cover all fields of autograph collecting. Members receive the quarterly journal *"Manuscripts"*, and have the opportunity to attend an annual convention held each May.

You can contact them at:
The Manuscript Society
350 N. Niagara St.
Burbank, CA 91505-3648

The Manuscript Society

KISS ME KATE

Sometimes the hallmark of a great collection is its uniqueness. A few collectors have built interesting lip print collections by asking their favorite star to lipstick up, pucker onto a page, and sign. As you can see, men have done it too!

CANDICE BERGEN

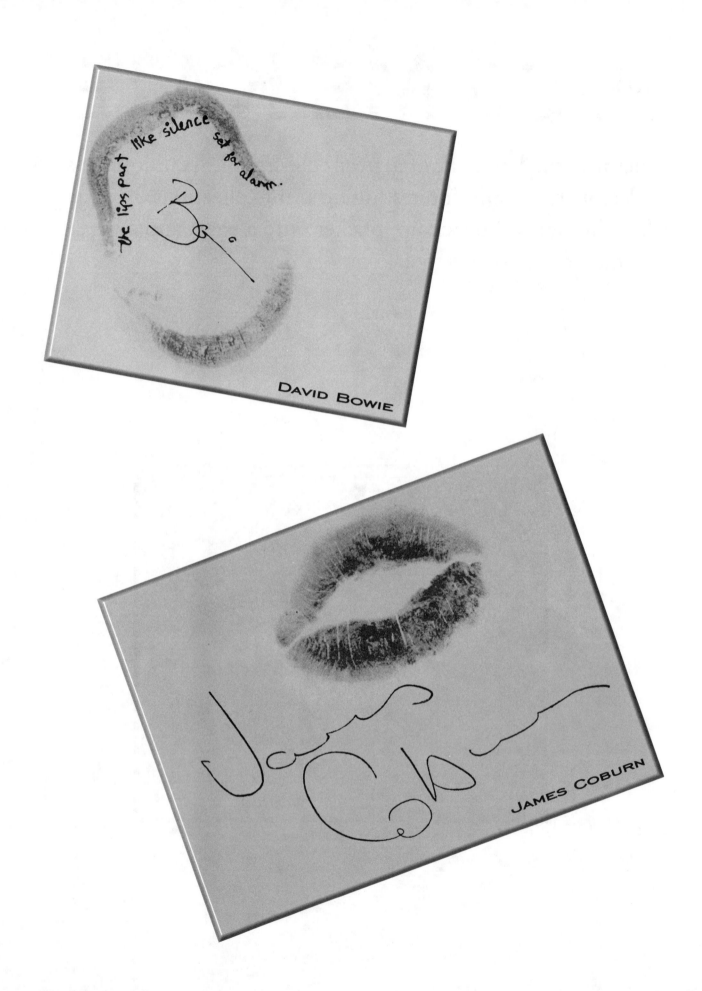

The lips part like silence set for alarm.

DAVID BOWIE

JAMES COBURN

Love and XXXs
Joan Collins

JOAN COLLINS

excuse the smudge, its
my first time (with a piece...
of paper)

Sean Connery

SEAN CONNERY

BETTE DAVIS

MARLENE DIETRICH

Virgin Kisses! Almost!

With my best wishes!

Kirk Douglas

KIRK DOUGLAS

Love Lesley-Anne Down

LESLEY - ANNE DOWN

DOUGLAS FAIRBANKS

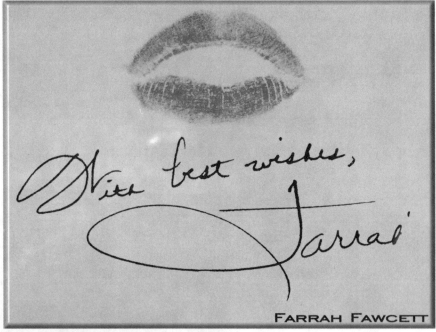

FARRAH FAWCETT

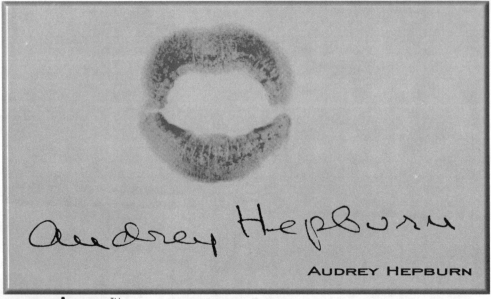

AUDREY HEPBURN

ANJELICA HUSTON

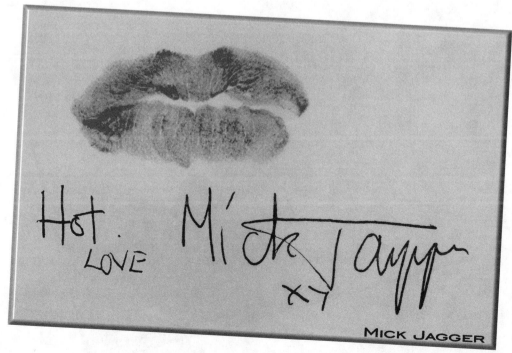

Hot.

LOVE

MICK JAGGER

SOPHIA LOREN

MALCOLM MACDOWELL

OLIVIA NEWTON-JOHN

OMAR SHARIF

ELIZABETH TAYLOR

MAE WEST

Signatures
A-Z

A

Bud Abbott &
Lou Costello

Paula Abdul

Brooke adams

Don Adams

85

Bryan Adams

Edie Adams

JULIE ADAMS

JULIE ADAMS
(B)

MAUDE ADAMS

SHARON ADAR

JOHN AGAR

CHARLES AIDMAN

DANNY AIELLO

EDWARD ALBEE

EDDIE ALBERT

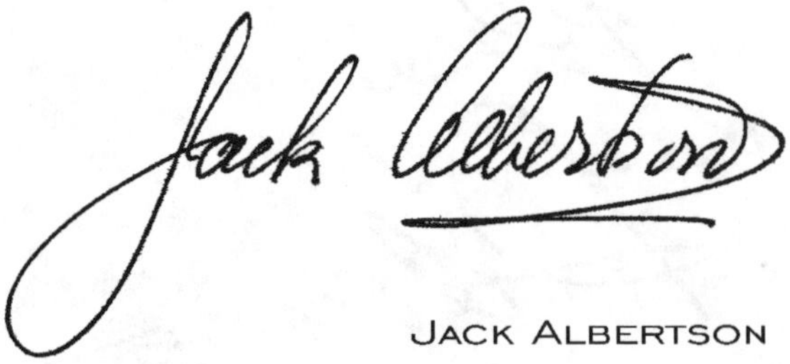

JACK ALBERTSON

KIM ALEXIS

DEBBIE ALLEN

MARCUS ALLEN

STEVE ALLEN

TIM ALLEN

TIM ALLEN(B)

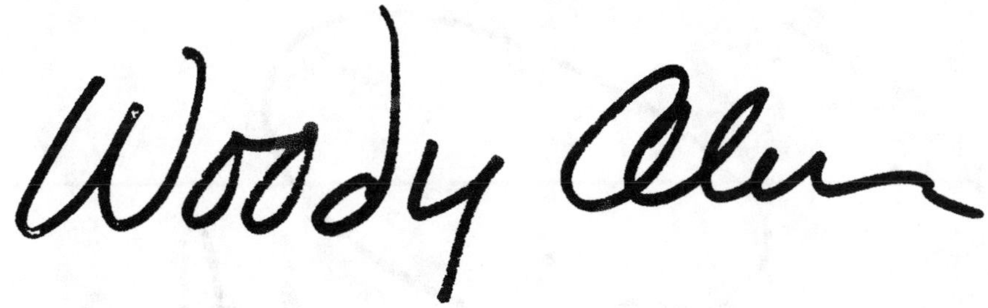

WOODY ALLEN

HERB ALPERT

CAROL ALT

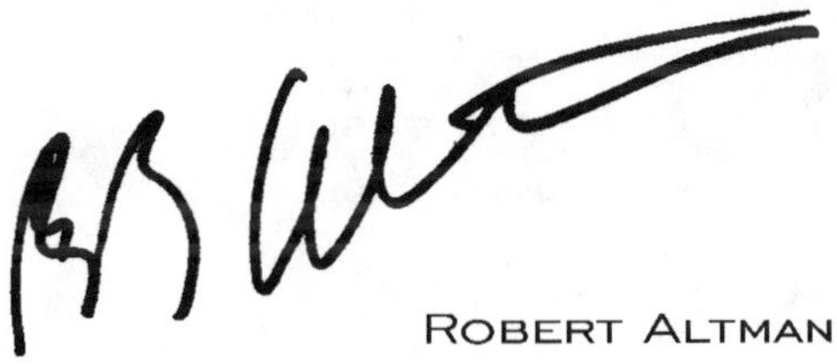

ROBERT ALTMAN

JOHN AMOS

MOREY AMSTERDAM

GILLIAN ANDERSON

LORI ANDERSON

PAMELA ANDERSON

RICHARD DEAN ANDERSON

RICHARD DEAN ANDERSON

Best wishes

Adam Ant

ADAM ANT

APOLLONIA

CHRISTINA APPLEGATE

ROSCOE FATTY ARBUCKLE

ANNE ARCHER

JOAN VAN ARK

LOUIS ARMSTRONG

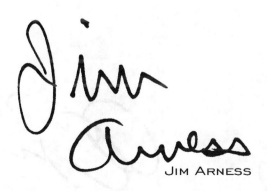

JIM ARNESS

DESI ARNAZ, JR.

EDDY ARNOLD

EDDY ARNOLD

TOM ARNOLD

ROSANNA ARQUETTE

ELIZABETH ASHLEY

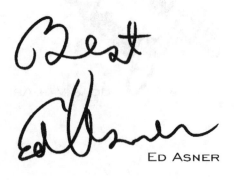

ED ASNER

ED ASNER

ARMAND ASSANTE

FRED ASTAIRE

JOHN ASTIN

CHET ATKINS

RICHARD ATTENBOROUGH

CLAUDINE AUGER

VIVIAN AUSTIN

GENE AUTRY

FRANKIE AVALON

HOYT AXTON

DAN AYKROYD

B

BABY FACE

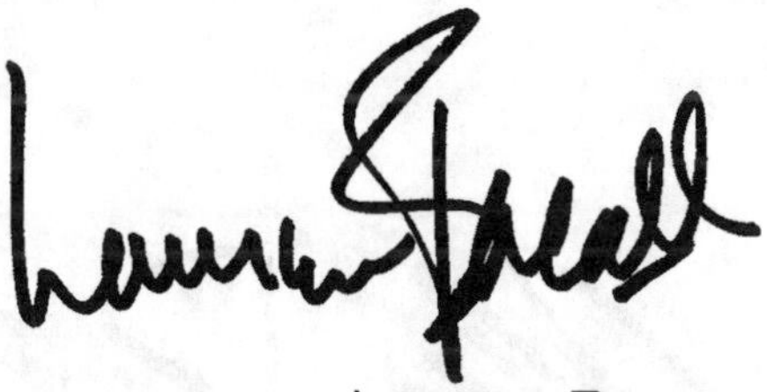

LAUREN BACALL

CATHERINE BACH

KEVIN BACON

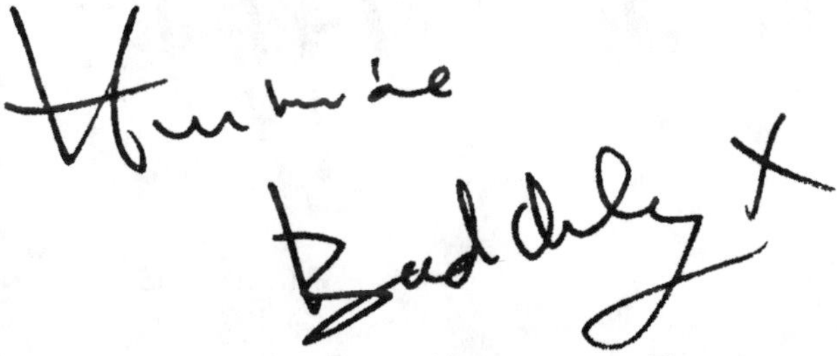

HERMIONE BADDELY

MAX BAER

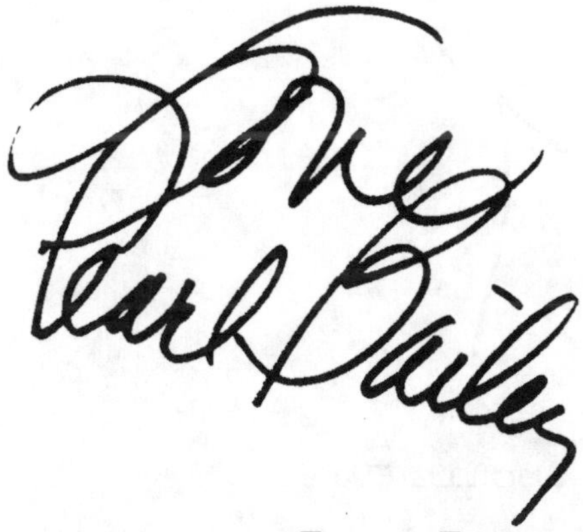

PEARL BAILEY

SCOTT BAIO

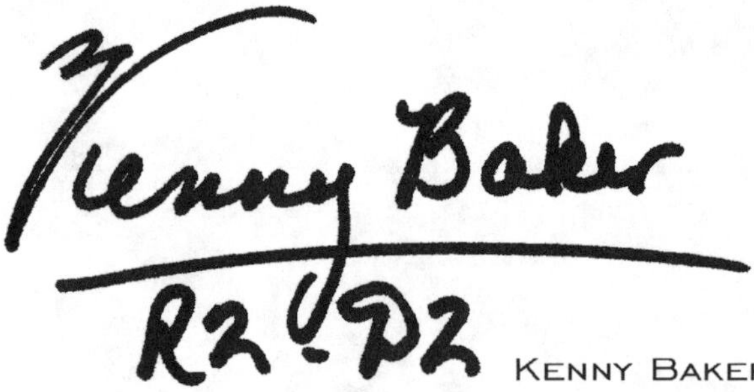

Kenny Baker

R2 D2

KENNY BAKER

SCOTT BAKULA

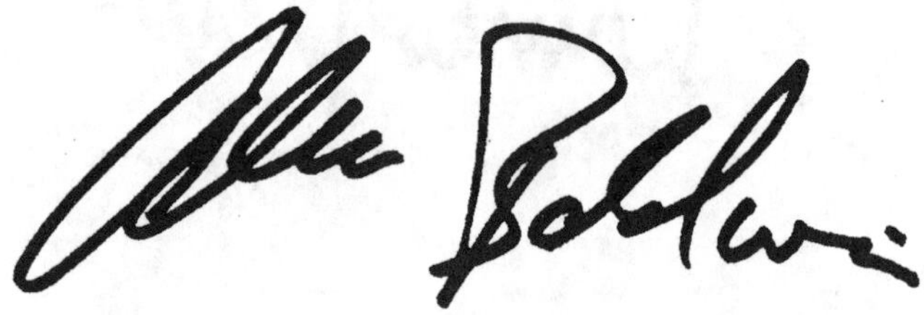

ALEC BALDWIN

PETER BALDWIN

STEPHEN BALDWIN

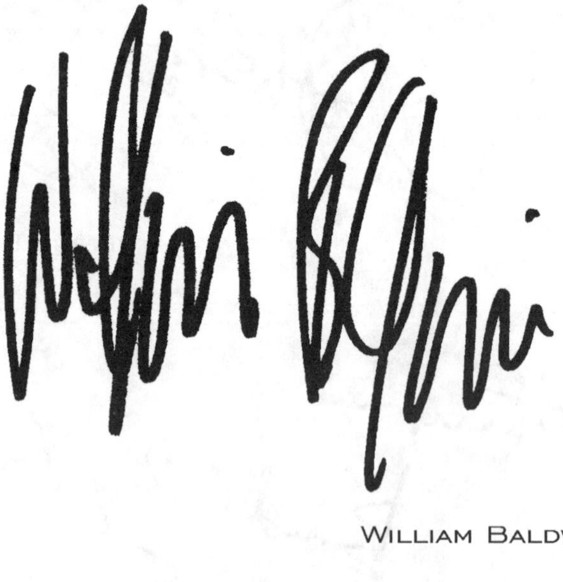

WILLIAM BALDWIN

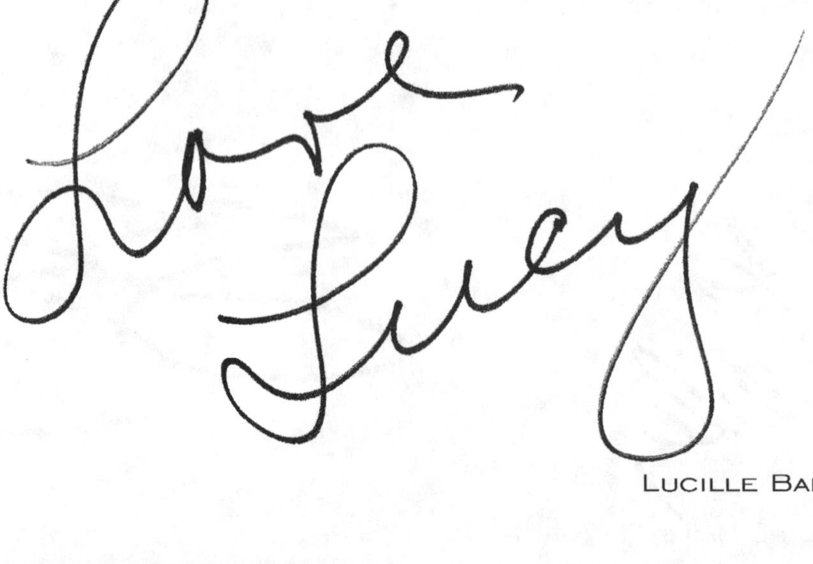

Love Lucy

LUCILLE BALL

ANNE BANCROFT

TYRA BANKS

PETE BARBUTTI

MAJEL BARRETT

DREW BARRYMORE

JOHN BARRYMORE

BILLY BARTY

TONI BASIL

JUSTINE BATEMAN

JASON BATEMAN

ALAN BATES

KATHY BATES

LES BAXTER

MEREDITH BAXTER - BIRNEY

MEREDITH BAXTER

ELGIN BAYLOR

ORSON BEAN

NED BEATTY

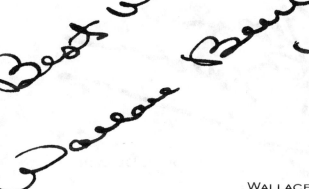

WARREN BEATY

MICHAEL BECK

WALLACE BEERY

ED BEGLEY, JR.

ED BEGLEY, SR.

SHARI BELAFONTE

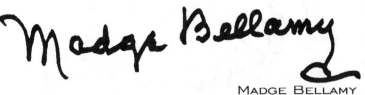

MADGE BELLAMY

JAMES BELUSHI

JACK BENNY

GEORGE BENSON

EDGAR BERGEN

INGRID BERGMAN

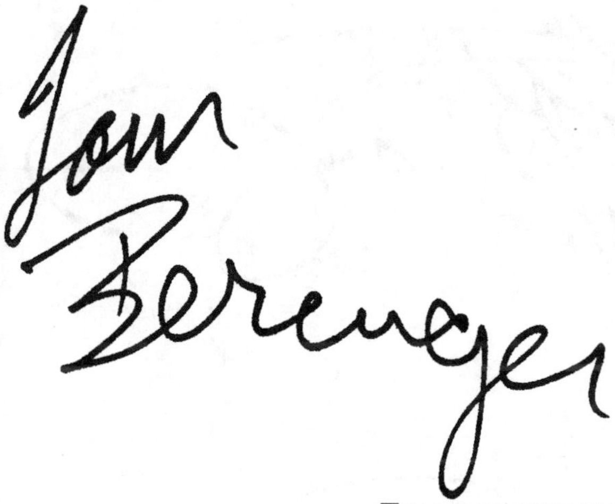

TOM BERENGER

ELIZABETH BERKLEY

MILTON BERLE

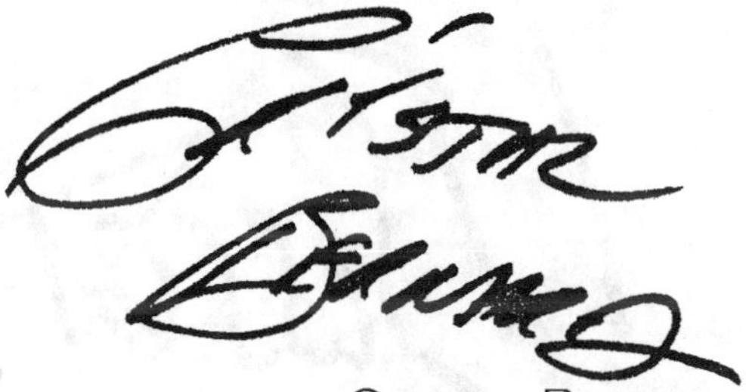

CRISTAL BERNARD

SANDRA BERNHARD

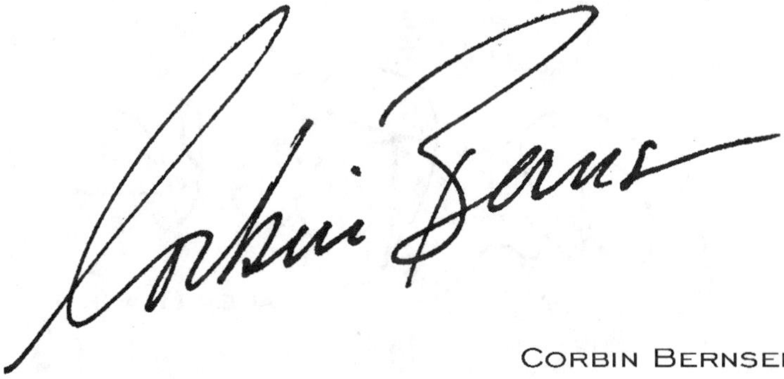

CORBIN BERNSEN

HALLE BERRY

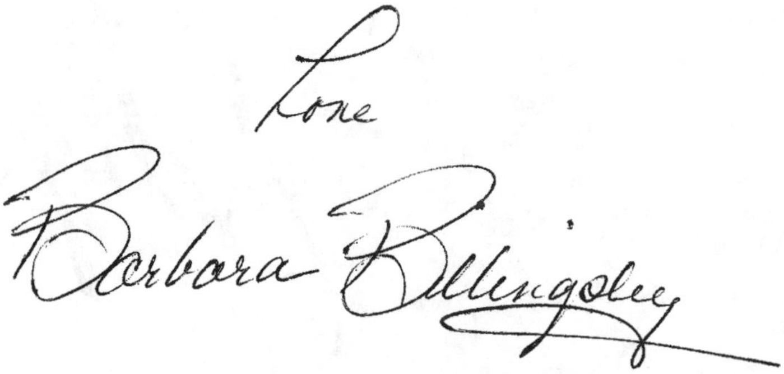

BARBARA BILLINGSLEY

JULIETTE BINOCHE

STEPHEN BISHOP

JAQUELINE BISSET

BILL BIXBY

KAREN BLACK

HONOR BLACKMAN

SALLY BLAINE

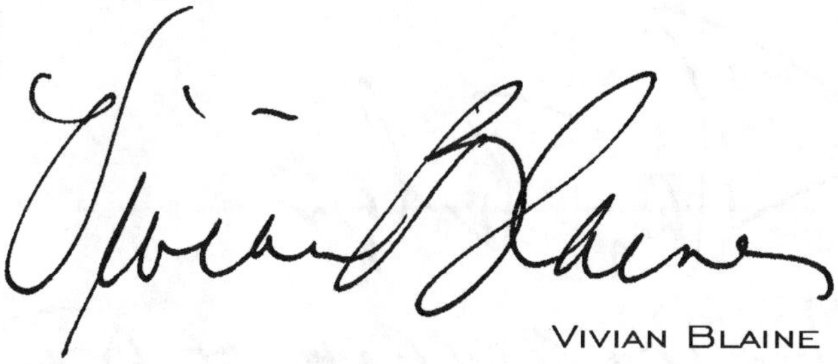

VIVIAN BLAINE

LINDA BLAIR

MEL BLANC

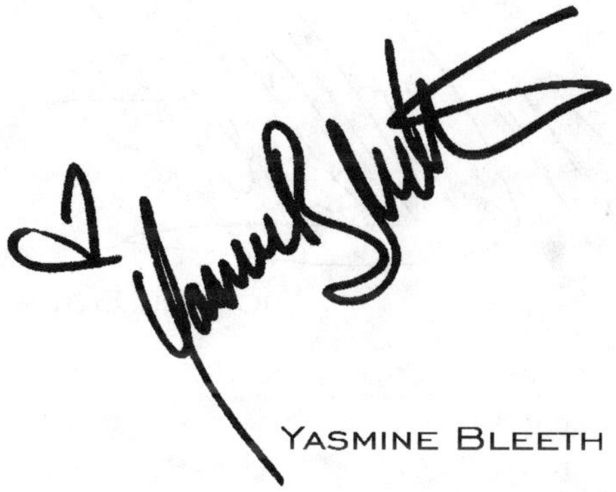

YASMINE BLEETH

BRENDA BLETHYN

BRIAN BLOOM

LISA BLOUNT

ANNE BLYTH

STEVEN BOCHCO

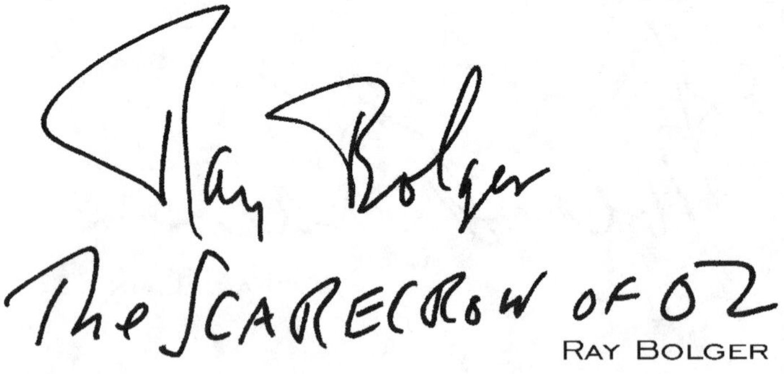

RAY BOLGER
THE SCARECROW OF OZ

MICHAEL BOLTON

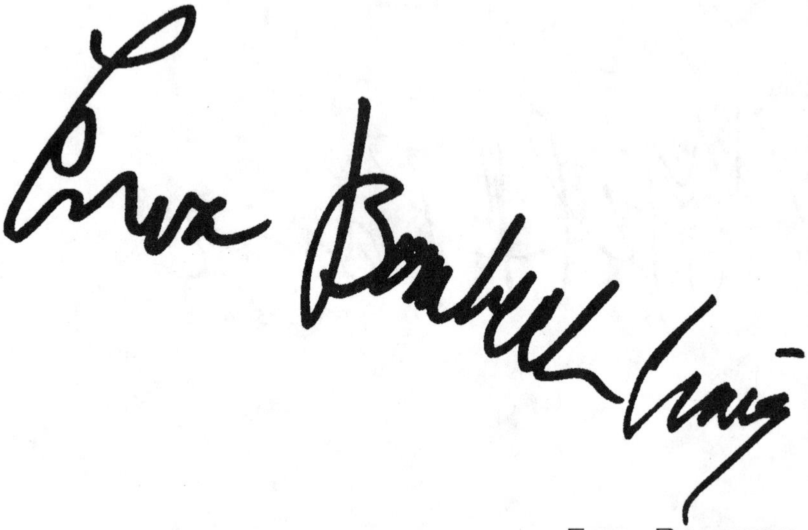

ERMA BOMBECK

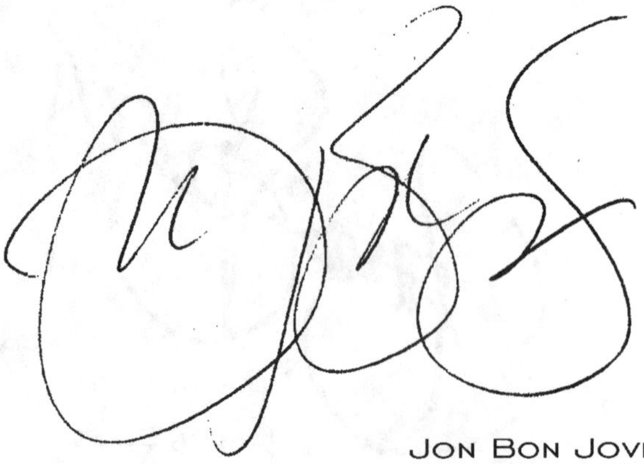

JON BON JOVI

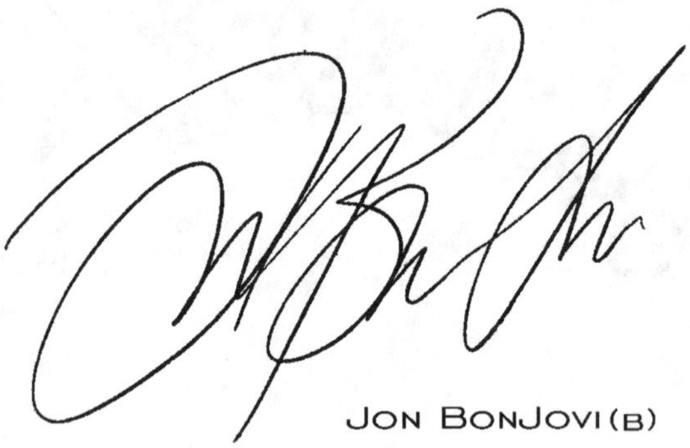

JON BONJOVI (B)

RICHARD BOONE

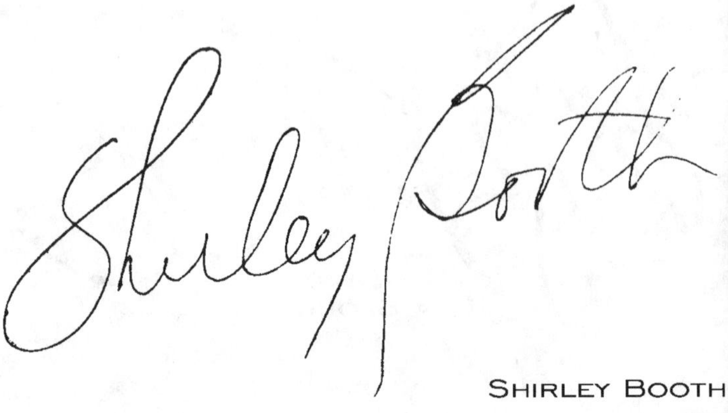

SHIRLEY BOOTH

ERNEST BORGNINE

BARBARA BOUCHETTE

BOBBIE BRESEE

CLARA BOW

DAVID BOWIE

CHRISTOPHER BOWMAN

BILL "HOPALONG CASSIDY" BOYD

LARA FLYNN BOYLE

PETER BOYLE

RAY BRADBURY

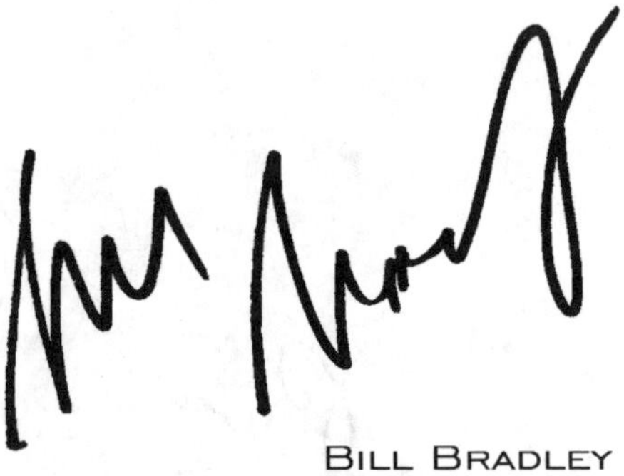

BILL BRADLEY

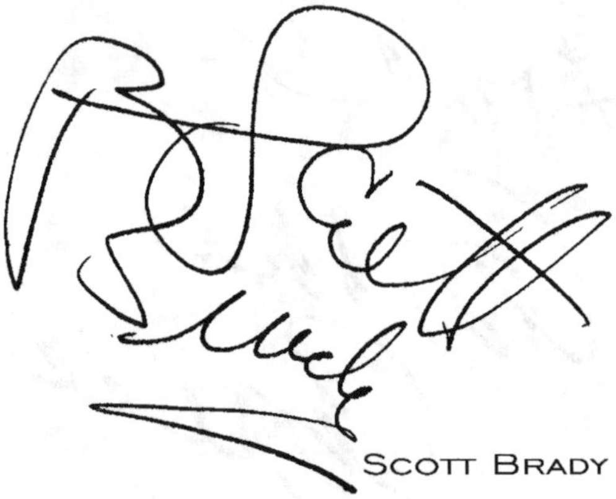

SCOTT BRADY

KENNETH BRANAGH

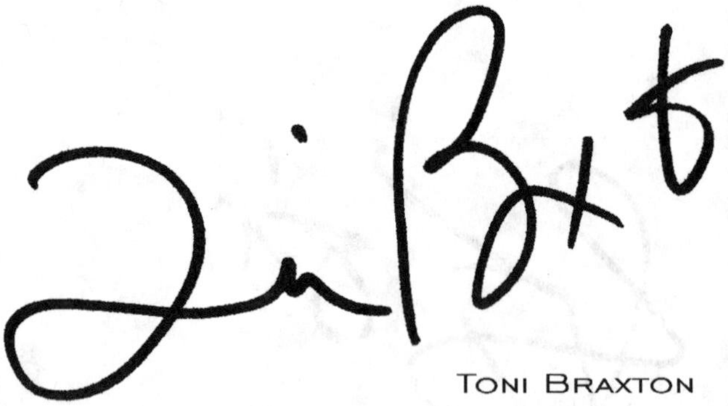

TONI BRAXTON

EILEEN BRENNAN

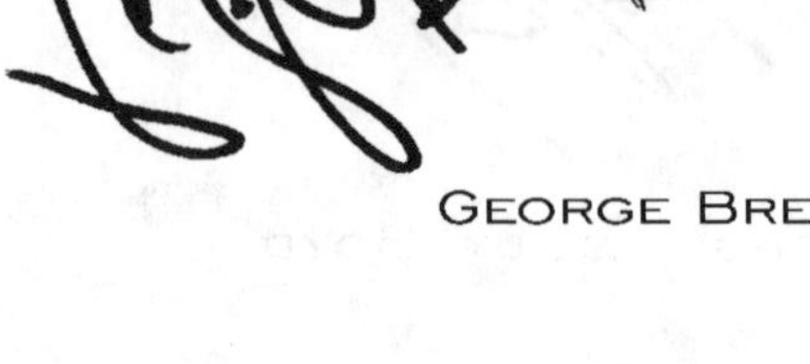

GEORGE BRETT

BEAU BRIDGES

BEAU BRIDGES (B)

LLOYD BRIDGES

MORGAN BRITTANY

MATTHEW BRODERICK

MATTHEW BRODERICK (B)

CHARLES BRONSON

MEL BROOKS

RAND BROOKS

RANDI BROOKS

PIERCE BROSNAN

JOYCE BROTHERS

RICOU BROWNING

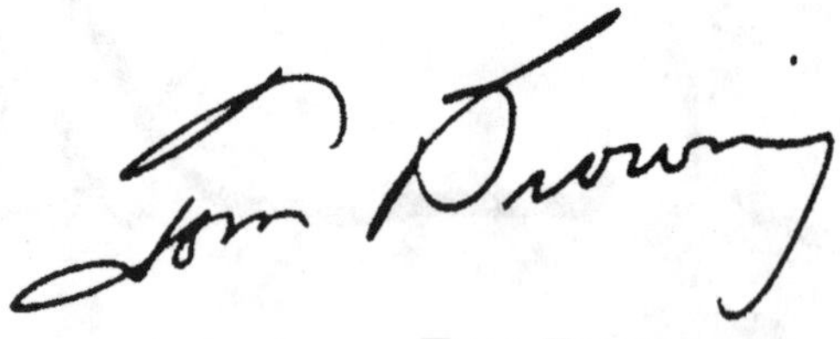

TOM BROWNING

PETER BROWN

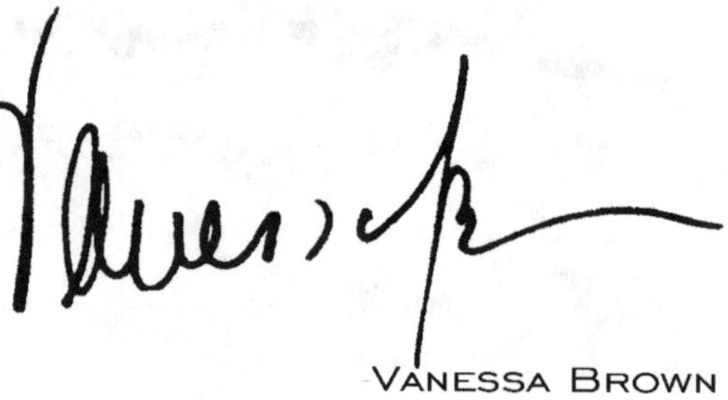

VANESSA BROWN

CAROL BURNETT(B)

CAROL BURNETT

GEORGE BURNS

GEORGE BURNS &
GRACIE ALLEN

RAYMOND BURR

ELLEN BURSTYN

LEVAR BURTON

LEVAR BURTON

RICHARD BURTON

TIM BURTON

STEVE BUSCEMI

BRETT BUTLER

RED BUTTONS

TIM BUTTONS

EDD BYRNES

C

JAMES CAAN

SID CAESAR

NICOLAS CAGE

JAMES CAGNEY

JEANNE CAGNEY

DEAN CAIN

MICHAEL CAINE

God Bless

KIRK CAMERON

GLEN CAMPBELL

NAOMI CAMPBELL

RAFAEL CAMPOS

MARY GRACE CANFIELD

DYAN CANNON

CLAUDIA CARDINALE

DREW CAREY

MARIAH CAREY

Entertainment Edition

RON CAREY

JOHN CARPENTER

TIA CARRERE

CARROT TOP

DANA CARVEY

JOHNNY CASH

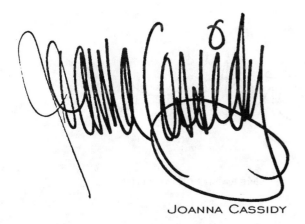

JOANNA CASSIDY

SEAN CASSIDY

PHOBE CATES

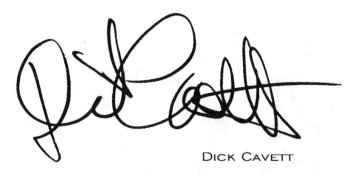

DICK CAVETT

RICHARD CHAMBERLAIN

RICHARD CHAMBERLAIN (B)

CAROL CHANNING

CHARLIE CHAPLIN

MELANIE CHARTOFF

DAVID CHARVET

BARRIE CHASE

CHER

LOIS CHILES

TODD CHRISTENSEN

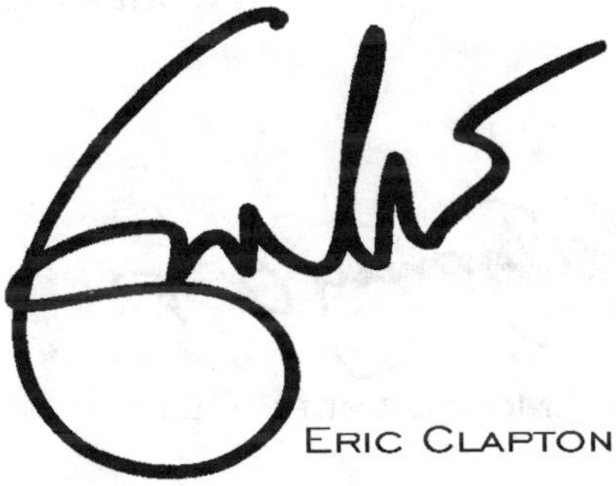

ERIC CLAPTON

All the best
Cindy Clark
American Graffiti

CANDY CLARK

MAE CLARKE

ROY CLARK

ROBERT CLARY

ANDREW DICE CLAY

MONTGOMERY CLIFT

PATSY CLINE

GEORGE CLOONEY

GEORGE CLOONEY(B)

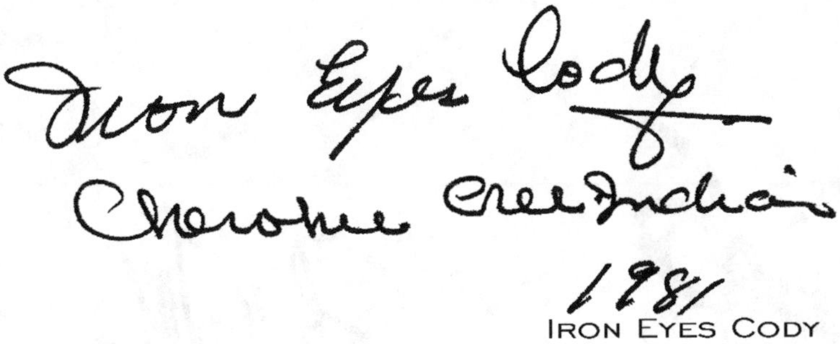

Iron Eyes Cody

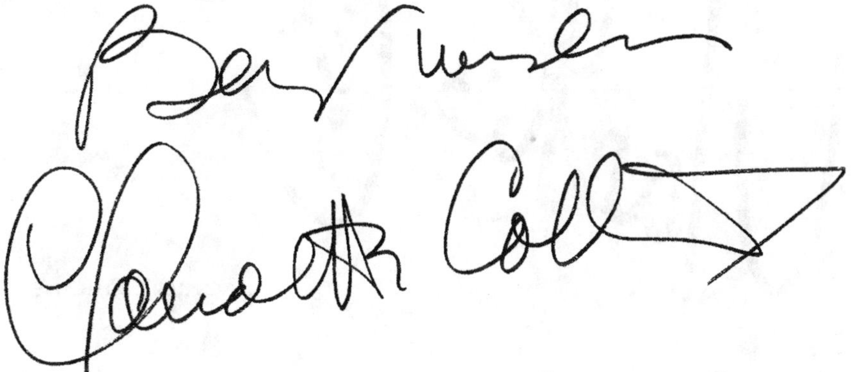

Cherokee Cree Indian

1981

IRON EYES CODY

CLAUDETTE COLBERT

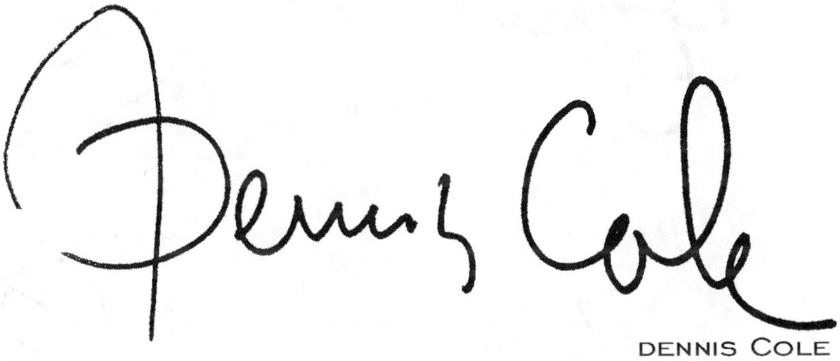

DENNIS COLE

JAMES COBURN

DABNEY COLEMAN

Love NATALIE COLE

JACKIE COLLINS

STEPHEN COLLINS

JESSI COLTER

PHIL COLLINS

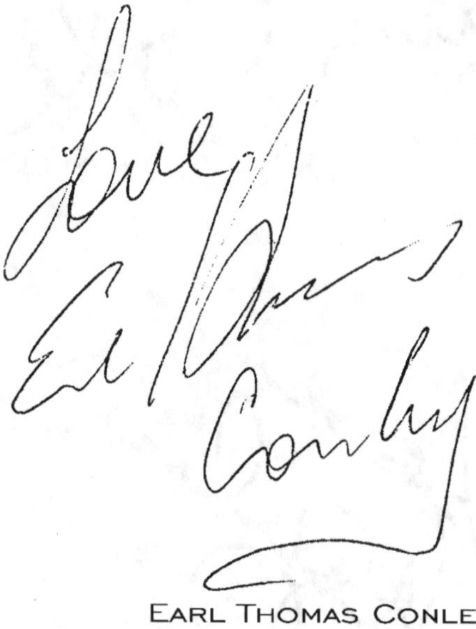

EARL THOMAS CONLEY

CAROL CONNERS

SEAN CONNERY

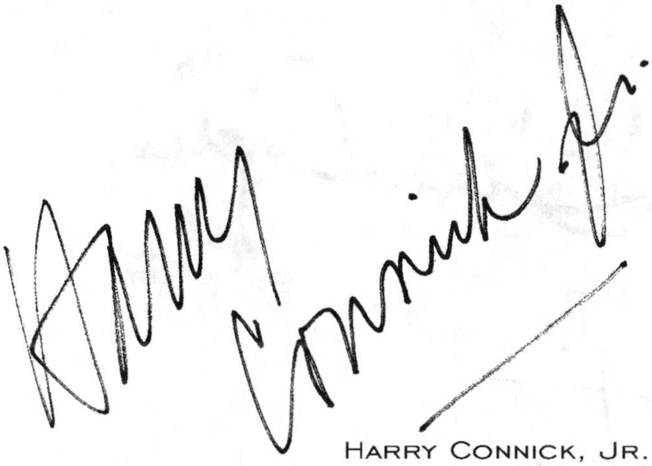

HARRY CONNICK, JR.

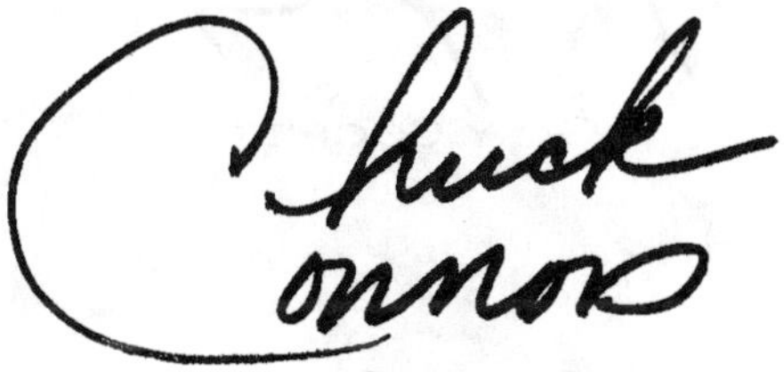

CHUCK CONNORS

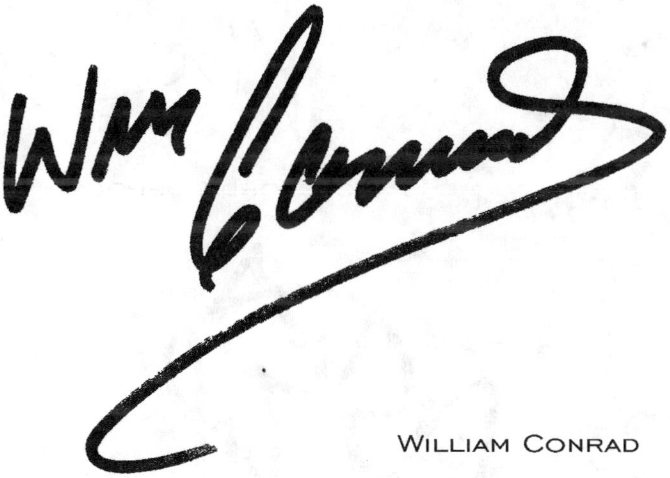

WILLIAM CONRAD

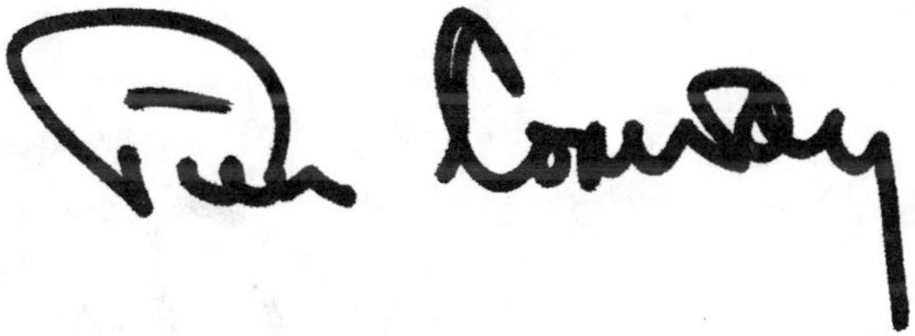

TIM CONWAY

JACKIE COOGAN

COOLIO

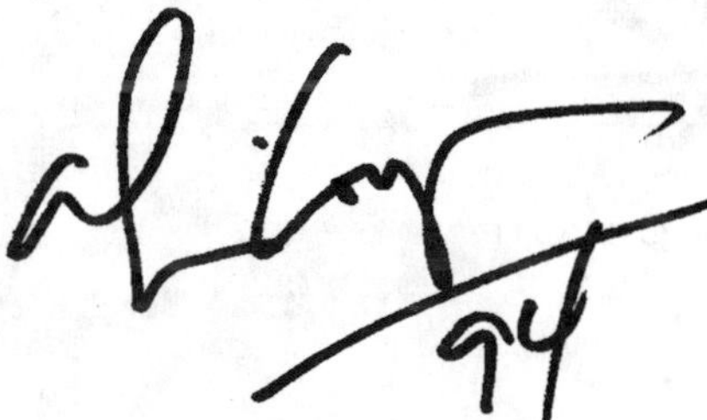

ALICE COOPER

GARY COOPER

TERI COPLEY

DAVID COPPERFIELD

FRANCIS FORD COPPOLA

BILL COSBY

COURTENEY COX

PETER COYOTE

Loads of luck

BUSTER CRABBE

WES CRAVEN

JOAN CRAWFORD

MICHAEL CRAWFORD

MICHAEL CRICHTON

JAMES CROMWELL

BING CROSBY

KATHRYN GRANT CROSBY

TOM CRUISE

BILLY CRYSTAL

MCCAULEY CULKIN

ROBERT CULP

TIM CURRY

KEN CURTIS

TONY CURTIS

BILLY RAY CYRUS (B)

JOHN CUSACK

BILLY RAY CYRUS

D

Timothy Dalton (signature)

TIMOTHY DALTON

Claire Danes (signature)

CLAIRE DANES

Rodney Dangerfield (signature)

RODNEY DANGERFIELD

Jeff Daniels (signature)

JEFF DANIELS

Tony Danza (signature)

TONY DANZA

Jean Darling (signature)

JEAN DARLING

Robert Davi (signature)

ROBERT DAVI

Bette Davis (signature)

BETTE DAVIS

BRAD DAVIS

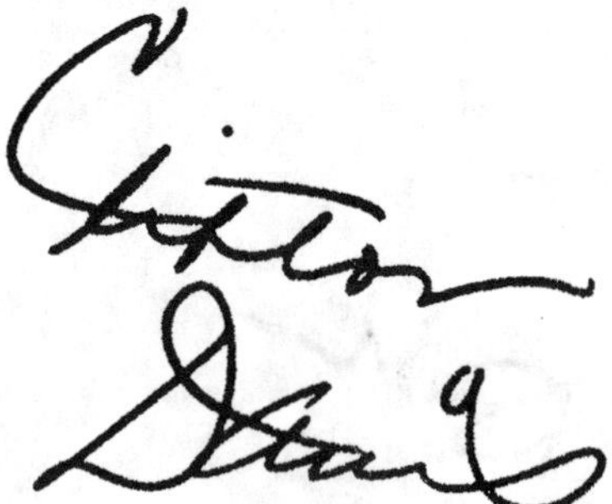

CLIFTON DAVIS

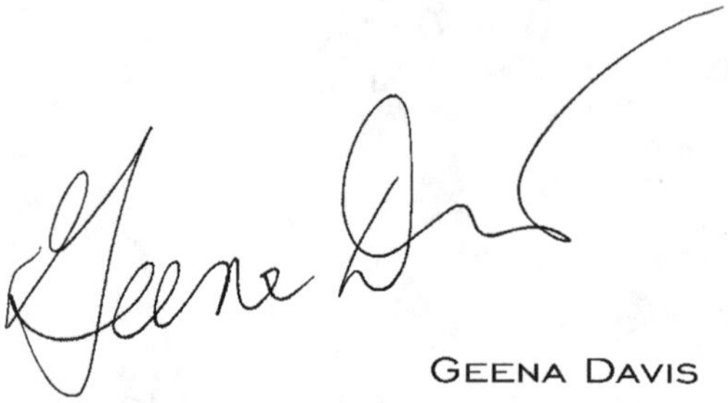

GEENA DAVIS

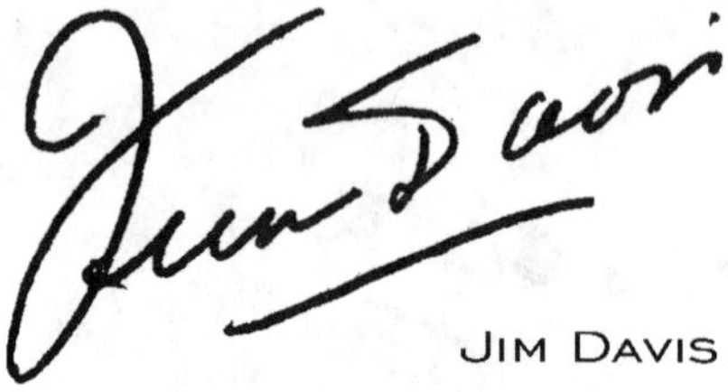

JIM DAVIS

SAMMY DAVIS, JR.

WARWICK DAVIS

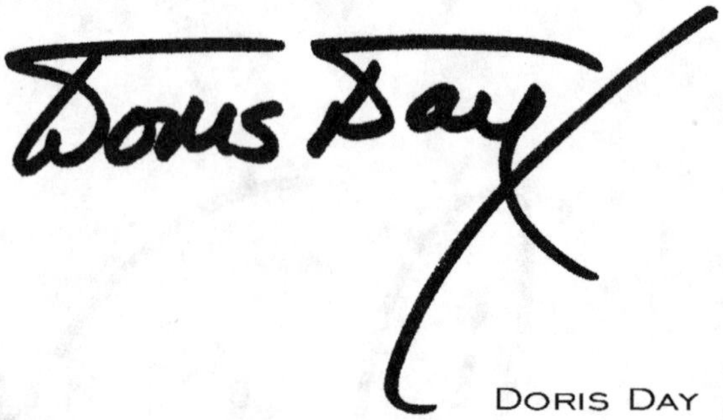

PAM DAWBER

DORIS DAY

DENNIS DAY

Very Best Wishes.

OLIVIA DE HAVILLAND

JONATHAN DEMME

JAMES DEAN

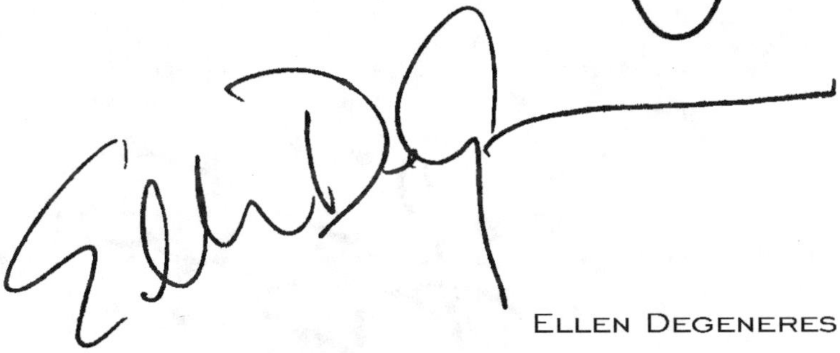

ELLEN DEGENERES

JULIE DELPY

love

REBECCA DeMORNAY

PATRICK DEMPSEY

PATRICK DEMPSEY

BRIAN DENNEHY

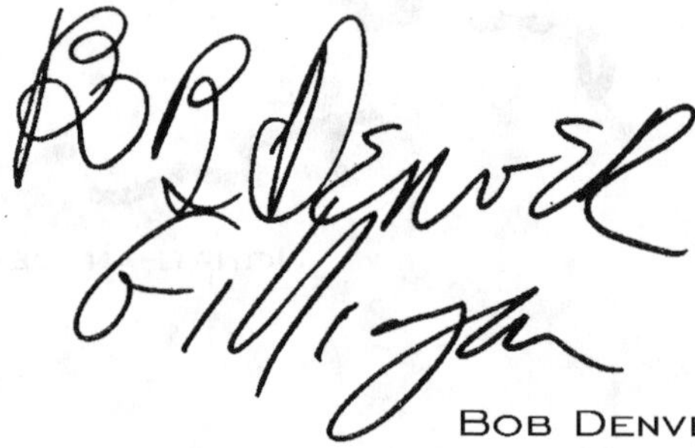

BOB DENVER

JOHN DENSMORE

LAURA DERN

DANNY DEVITO

SUSAN DEY

Leonardo DiCaprio
(early signature)

Leonardo DiCaprio

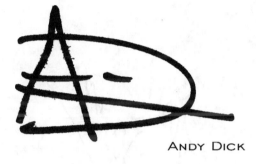

Andy Dick

Angie Dickinson

Eric Dickerson

Marlene Dietrich

Phyllis Diller

Kevin Dillon

MATT DILLON

CELINE DION

WALT DISNEY

DIVINE

SHANNEN DOHERTY

AMI DOLENZ

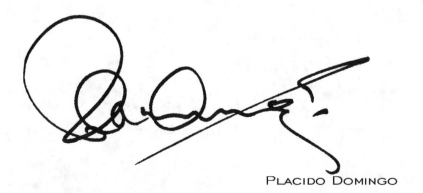

PLACIDO DOMINGO

PLACIDO DOMINGO(B)

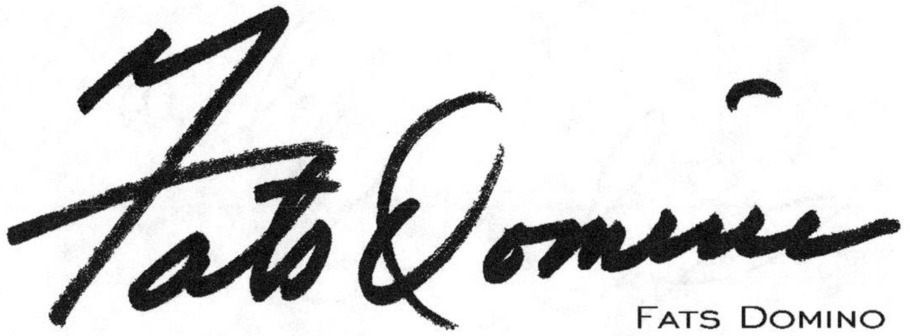

FATS DOMINO

PHIL DONAHUE

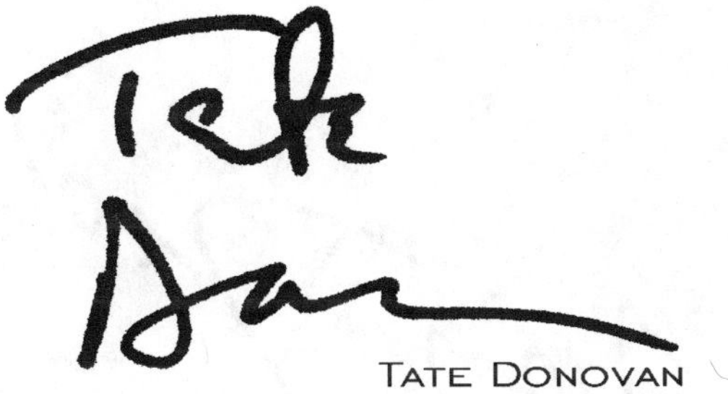

TATE DONOVAN

PHIL DONAHUE

JAMES DOOHAN

STEPHEN DORFF

KIRK DOUGLAS

KIRK DOUGLAS (B)

MORTON DOWNEY, JR.

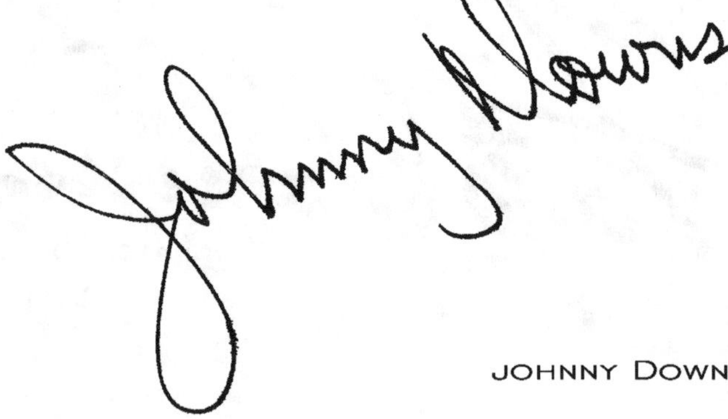

JOHNNY DOWNS

TONY DOW

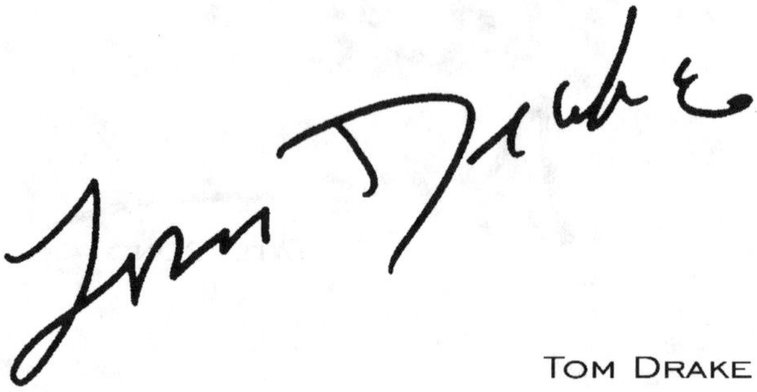

TOM DRAKE

FRAN DRESCHER

RICHARD DREYFUSS

DAVID DUCHOVNY

PATTY DUKE ASTIN

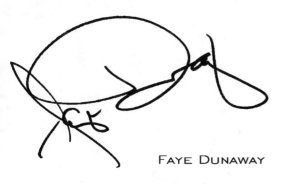

FAYE DUNAWAY

KIRSTEN DUNST

JIMMY DURANTE

ROBERT DUVALL

ROBERT DUVALL (B)

SHELLEY DUVAL

E

(signature)

ELIZABETH EARL

(signature)

SHEENA EASTON

(signature)

CLINT EASTWOOD
(EARLY)

Take care
(signature)
94

SHIRLEY EATON

(signature)

ROGER EBERT

BUDDY EBSEN

(signature)

BARBARA EDEN

ANTHONY EDWARDS

PENNY EDWARDS

NICOLE EGGERT

NICOLE EGGERT(B)

JILL EIKENBERRY

MICHAEL EISNER

BRITT EKLAND

ERIKA ELENIAK

CARMEN ELECTRA

HECTOR ELIZONDO

JOHN ELWAY

RON ELY

ROBERT ENGLUND

RON ELY
(B)

GREG EVIGAN

JANET EVANS

RUPERT EVERETT

F

DOUGLAS FAIRBANKS, JR.

JEFF FAHEY

CHRIS FARLEY

PETER FALK

RICHARD FARNSWORTH

MIKE FARRELL

ALICE FAYE

SHELLEY FABARES

COREY FELDMAN

COREY FELDMAN (YOUNG)

FEDERICO FELLINI

SHERILYN FENN

LOU FERRIGNO

SALLY FIELD

KIM FIELDS

W.C. FIELDS

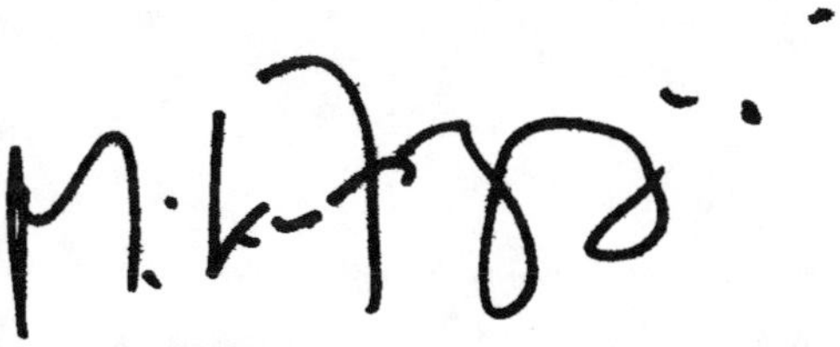

MIKE FIGGIS

PETER FINCH

CARRIE FISHER

ROBERTA FLACK

RHONDA FLEMING

LOUISE FLETCHER

CALISTA FLOCKHART

ERROL FLYNN

BRIDGET FONDA

HENRY FONDA

JANE FONDA

JANE FONDA(B)

PETER FONDA

JOAN FONTAINE

DAVID FOSTER

MILOS FORMAN

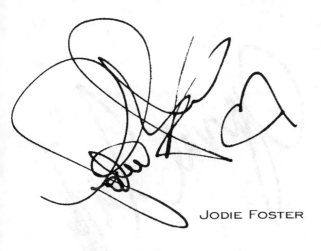

JODIE FOSTER

BERNARD FOX

SAMANTHA FOX

JONATHAN FRAKES

MARY FRANN

DENNIS FRANZ

Janie Fricke

JANIE FRICKE

Jonathan Frid

JONATHAN FRID

Soleil Moon Frye

SOLEIL MOON FRYE

G

[signature]

Eva Gabor

[signature]

Greta Garbo

Gallagher

[signature]

Gil Garcetti

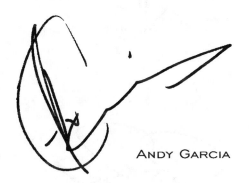

Andy Garcia

[signature]

Ava Gardner

[signature]

Randy Gardner

BEVERLY GARLAND

JAMES GARNER

PEGGY ANN GARNER

JANEANE GAROFALO

LEIF GARRETT

TERI GARR

TERI GARR (B)

GREER GARSON

JOHN GAVIN

MITZI GAYNOR

ANTHONY GEARY

CRYSTAL GAYLE

WILL GEER

CHRISTOPHER GEORGE

BALTHAZAR GETTY

ALICE GHOSTLEY

love —

DEBBIE GIBSON

HENRY GIBSON

92

MEL GIBSON

KATHIE LEE GIFFORD

MELISSA GILBERT

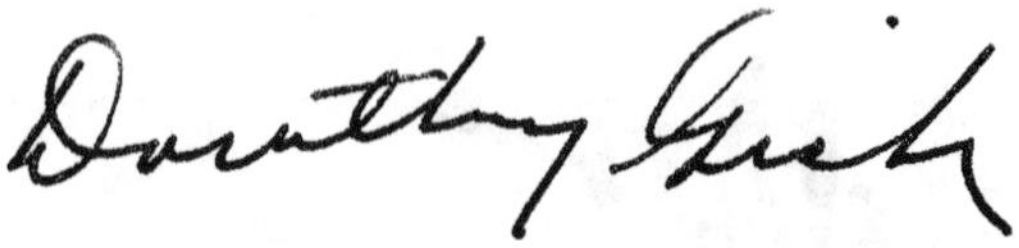

DOROTHY GISH

KENNY G

JACKIE GLEASON

SCOTT GLENN

SHARON GLESS

DANNY GLOVER

WHOOPI GOLDBERG

TRACEY GOLD

CUBA GOODING, JR.

JOHN GOODMAN

RUTH GORDON

GILBERT GOTTFRIED

ALEXANDER GODUNOV

ELLIOT GOULD

BETTY GRABEL

ROBERT GOULET

HEATHER GRAHAM

FARLEY GRANGER

CARY GRANT

HUGH GRANT

HUGH GRANT

LEE GRANT

PETER GRAVES

GIL GERARD

SIDNEY GREENSTREET

JENNIFER GREY

JOEL GREY (B)

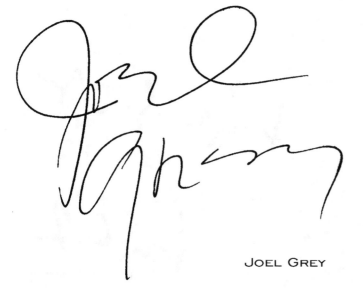

JOEL GREY

PAM GRIER

RICHARD GRECCO

CHARLES GRODIN

MICHAEL GROSS

ROBERT GUILLAUME

ALEC GUINNESS

STEVE GUTTENBERG

JASMINE GUY

EDMUND GWENN

H

LARRY HAGMAN

COREY HAIM

ARSENIO HALL

DEIDRE HALL

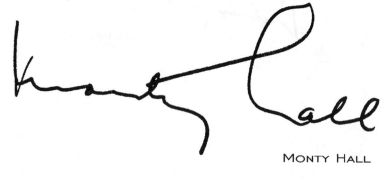

MONTY HALL

BRETT HALSEY

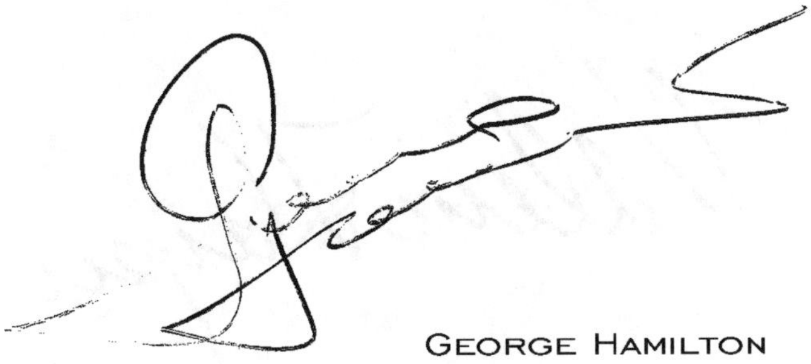

GEORGE HAMILTON

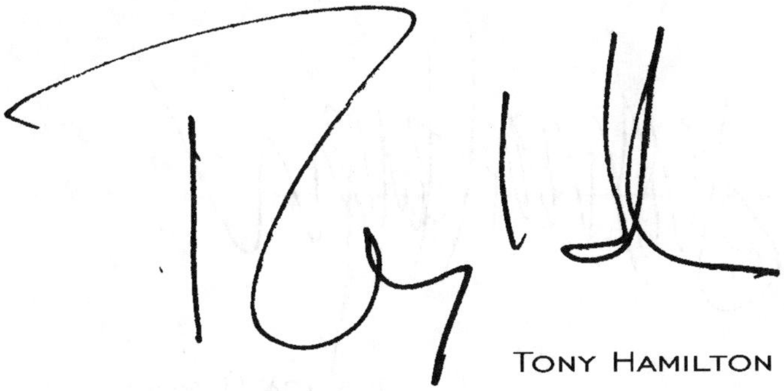

TONY HAMILTON

HARRY HAMLIN

MARVIN HAMLISCH

HERBIE HANCOCK

TOM HANKS

PAGE HANNAH

JEAN HARLOW

JESSICA HARPER

VALERIE HARPER

WOODY HARRELSON

ED HARRIS

MEL HARRIS

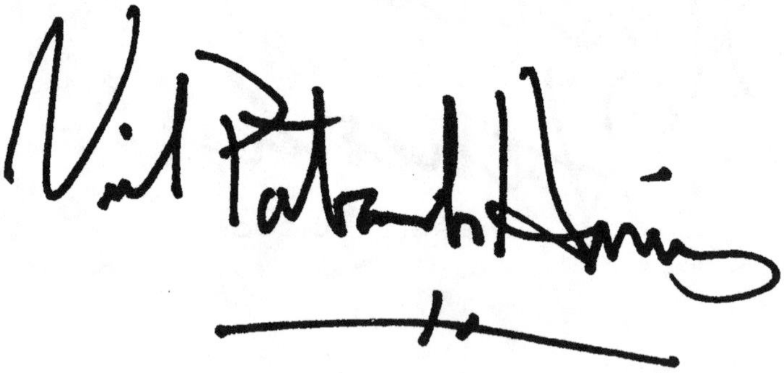

NEIL PATRICK HARRIS

JENNILEE HARRISON

SAM HARRIS

JACKEE HARRY

MARIETTE HARTLEY

MELISSA JOAN HART

JASON HARVEY

PETER HASKELL

DAVID HASSELHOFF

LUCAS HASS (KID)

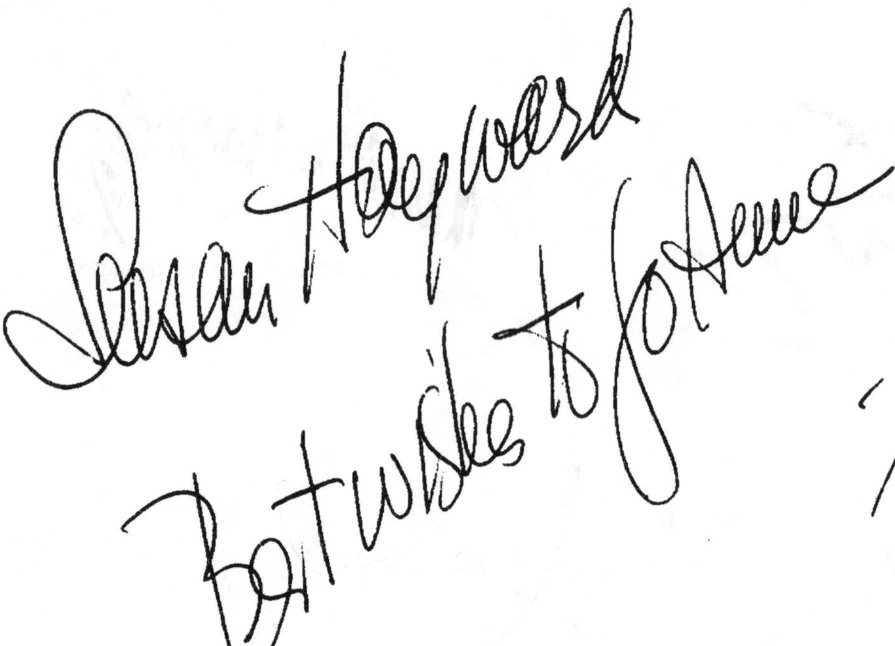

SUSAN HAYWARD

RITA HAYWORTH

MARTY HAZZARD

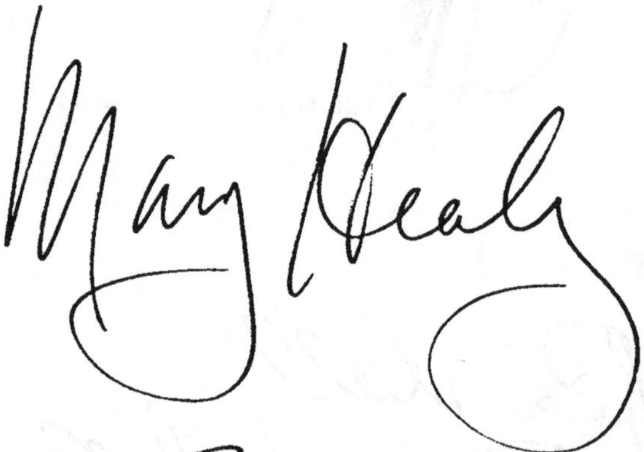

MARY HEALY

THOMAS HEARN

JOHN HEARD

6-21-89

THOMAS HEARN (B)

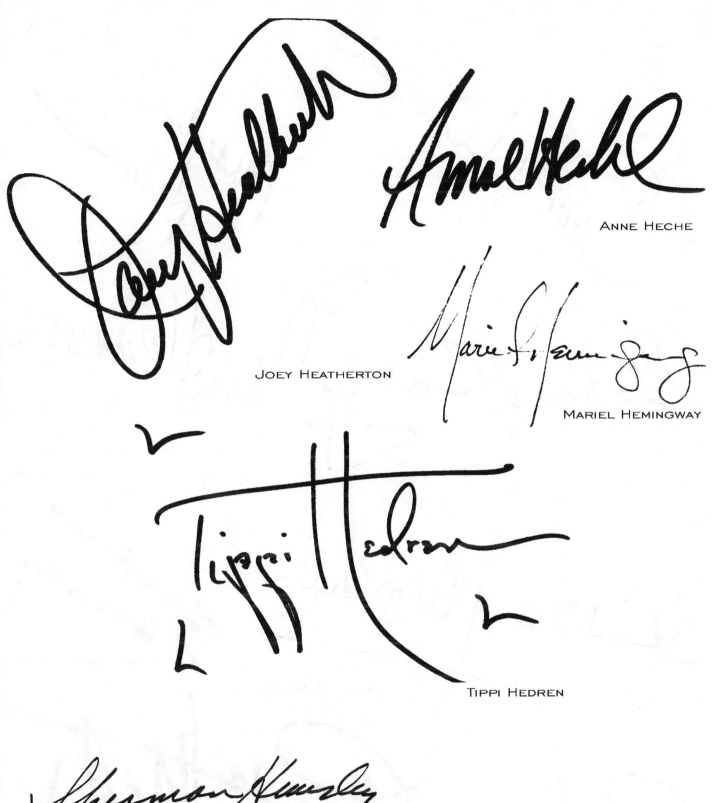

ANNE HECHE

JOEY HEATHERTON

MARIEL HEMINGWAY

TIPPI HEDREN

SHERMAN HEMSLEY

HUGH HEFNER

Jimi Hendrix signature

JIMI HENDRIX

Marilu Henner signature

MARILU HENNER

Gloria Henry signature

GLORIA HENRY

Jim Henson signature

JIM HENSON

Audrey Hepburn signature

AUDREY HEPBURN

Barbara Hershey signature

BARBARA HERSHEY

Charlton Heston (b) signature

CHARLTON HESTON(B)

Charlton Heston signature

CHARLTON HESTON

DWAYNE HICKMAN

JOHN HILLERMAN

HAL HOLBROOK

BOB HOPE

ANTHONY HOPKINS

ANTHONY HOPKINS(B)

RON HOWARD

ALFRED HITCHCOCK

SUSAN HOWARD

DAVID HUDDLESON

KATHLEEN HUGHES

JOHN HUGHES

JOHN HUNT

HELEN HUNT

ANJELICA HUSTON

OLIVIA HUSSEY

I

ICE T

BILLY IDOL

MARTY INGELS

JEREMY IRONS

AMY IRVING

J

Glenda Jackson

GLENDA JACKSON

JANET JACKSON

Jermaine Jackson

JERMAINE JACKSON

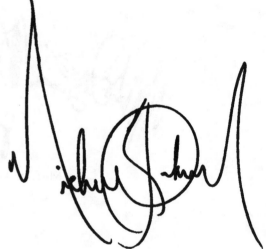

MICHAEL JACKSON

SAMUEL L. JACKSON

VICTORIA JACKSON

VICTORIA JACKSON (B)

DEAN JAGGER

MICK JAGGER

JOHN JAMES

CONRAD JANIS

DAN JANSEN

FAMKE JANSSEN

BRUCE JENNER

MAREN JENSEN

JEWEL

BEN JOHNSON

DON JOHNSON

LAURA JOHNSON

MICHELLE JOHNSON

VAN JOHNSON

JAMES EARL JONES

Love and peace!

JAMES EARL JONES

QUINCY JONES

SHIRLEY JONES

JANIS JOPLIN

SHIRLEY JONES
(B)

LOUIS JORDAN

ELAINE JOYCE

WYNONNA JUDD

K

Madeline Kahn (signature)

MADELINE KAHN

Carol Kane (signature)

CAROL KANE

Kitty Kallen (signature)

KITTY KALLEN

Garson Kanin (signature)

GARSON KANIN

Alex Karras (signature)

ALEX KARRAS

Boris Karloff (signature)

BORIS KARLOFF

Casey Kasem (signature)

CASEY KASEM

STACY KEACH

BUSTER KEATON

RUBY KEELER

BRIAN KEITH

BRIAN KEITH(B)

DAVID KEITH

GRACE KELLY

GRACE DE MONACO

GENE KELLY

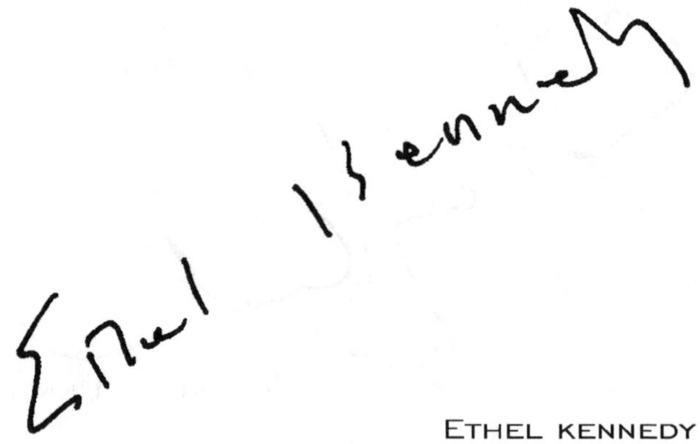

ETHEL KENNEDY

JOANNA KERNS

JAYNE KENNEDY

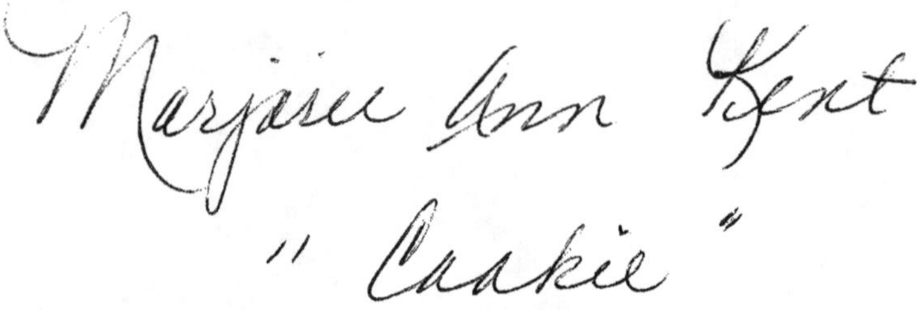

MARJORIE ANN KENT

JOHN KENNEDY, JR.

DEBORAH KERR

MARGOT KIDDER

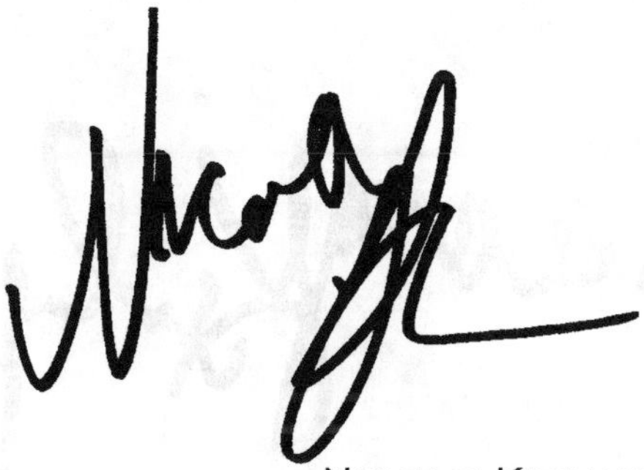

NICOLE KIDMAN

RICHARD KIEL

HARVEY KIETEL

VAL KILMER

LINCOLN KILPATRICK

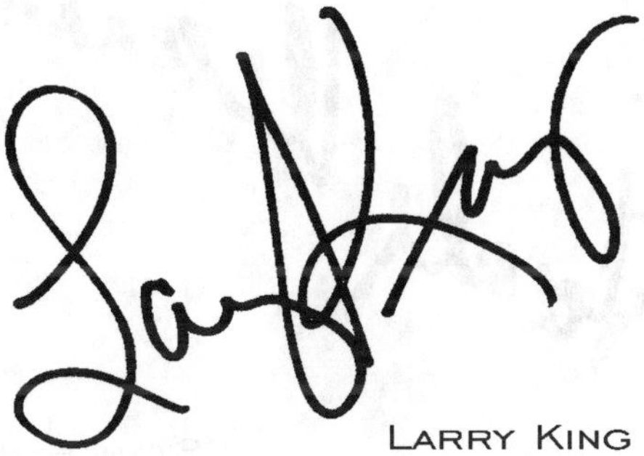

LARRY KING

MABEL KING

BEN KINGSLEY

GEORGE KIRBY

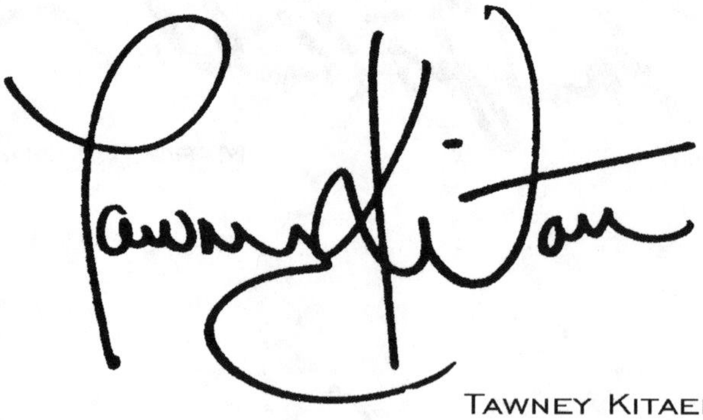

TAWNEY KITAEN

EARTHA KITT

JACK KLUGMAN

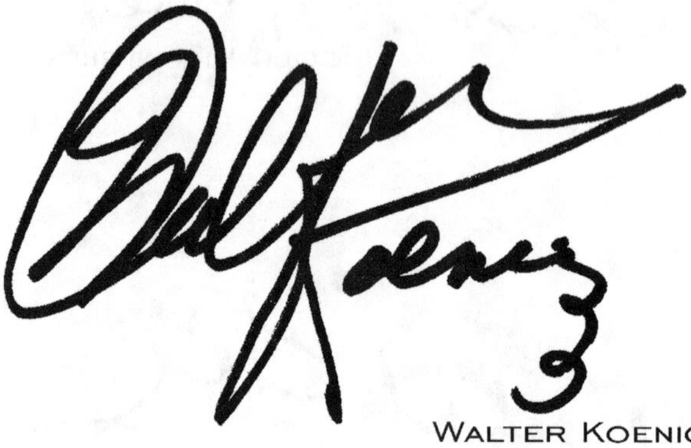

WALTER KOENIG

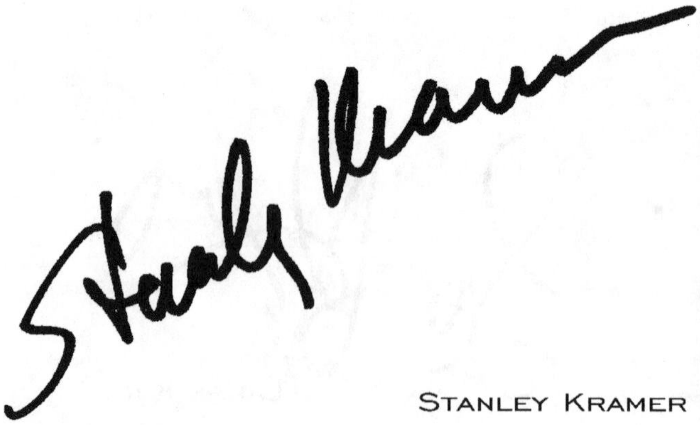

STANLEY KRAMER

STANLEY KRAMER (B)

JUDITH KRANTZ

LENNY KRAVITZ

TONY KUBEK

L

PATTI LaBELLE

ALAN LADD

CHERYL LADD

DIANE LADD

CHRISTINE LAHTI

CHRISTOPHER LAMBERT

DOROTHY LAMOUR

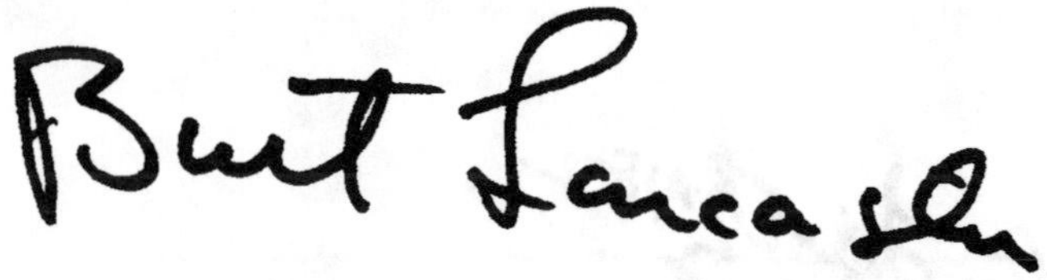

BURT LANCASTER

ELSA LANCHESTER

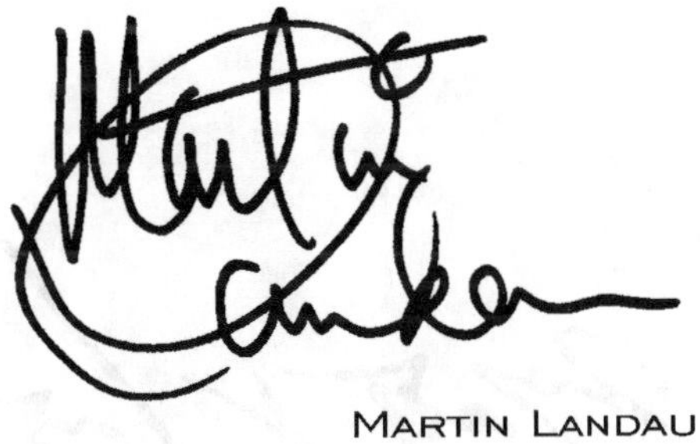

MARTIN LANDAU

ANN LANDERS

AUDREY LANDERS

JOE LANDO

JESSICA LANGE

K.D. LANG

WALTER LANTZ

JOE LARA

MATT LATANZI

LOUISE LATHAM

STAN LAUREL &
OLIVER HARDY

PIPER LAURIE

VICKI LAWRENCE

TIMOTHY LEARY

MATT LeBLANC

BRUCE LEE

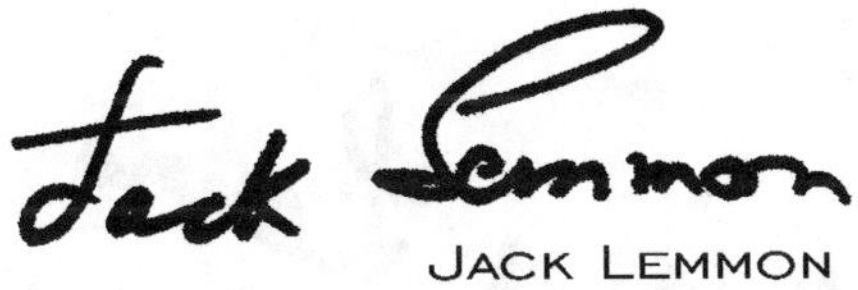

JACK LEMMON

JANET LEIGH

JULIAN LENNON

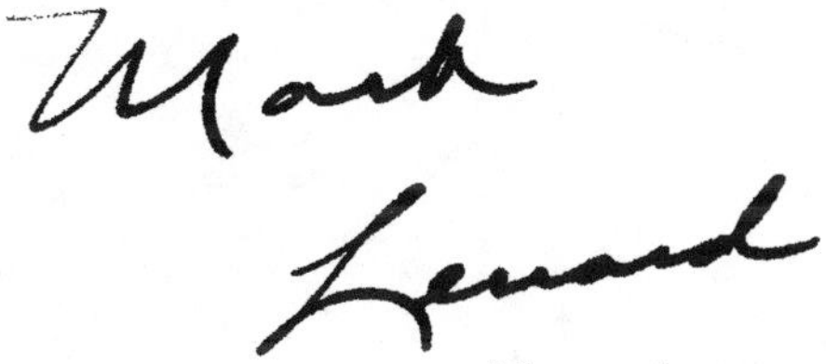

MARK LENARD

JAY LENO (B)

JAY LENO

MARION LESSING

BEN LESSY

DIANA LEWIS

HUEY LEWIS

JENNY LEWIS

MONICA LEWIS

LIBERACE

JOHN LEGUIZAMO

YVONNE LIME

JOHN LITHGOW

MARY LIVINGSTON

DESMOND LLEWELYN

HAROLD LLOYD

SONDRA LOCKE

ANNE LOCKHART

JOSH LOGAN

ROBERT LOGGIA

CAROLE LOMBARD

JULIE LONDON

MARJORIE LORD

SOPHIA LOREN

PETER LORRE

TINA LOUISE

JENNIFER LOVE-HEWITT

PAUL LUKAS

SUSAN LUCCI

BELA LUGOSI

PETER LUPUS

KELLY LYNCH

(B)
PETER LUPUS

JEFFREY LYNN

M

Marion Mack

MARION MACK

GAVIN MacLEOD

Dave Madden

DAVE MADDEN

Dave Madden

DAVE MADDEN(B)

MADONNA

VIRGINIA MADSEN

DEBRA SUE MAFFET

BILL MAHER

JOHN MALKOVICH

DOROTHY MALONE

HENRY MANCINI

JAYNE MANSFIELD

JERRY MAREN

MARGO

MARCEL MARCEAU

CHEECH MARIN

KAREN MORROW

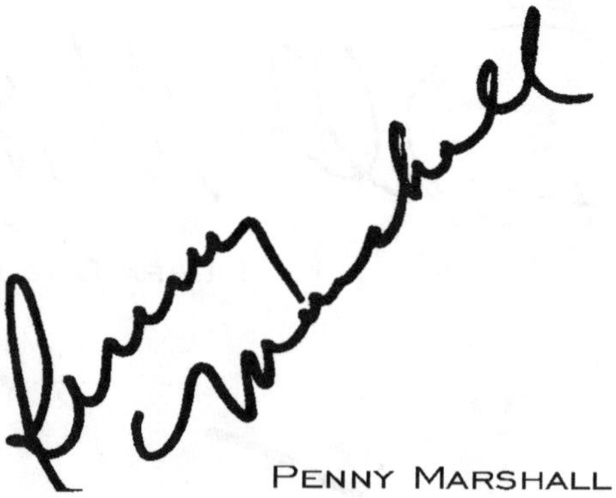

PENNY MARSHALL

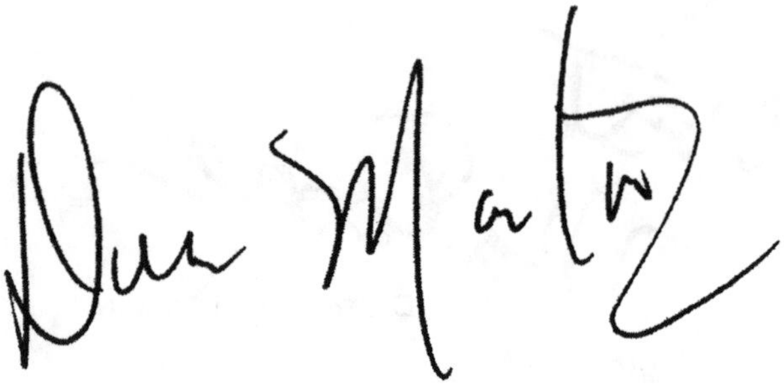

DEAN MARTIN

A. MARTINEZ

JARED MARTIN

KELLIE MARTIN

ROSS MARTIN

STEVE MARTIN

LEE MARVIN

Virginia Mayo (signature)

VIRGINIA MAYO

Groucho Marx (signature)

GROUCHO MARX

Chico Marx (signature)

CHICO MARX

Harpo Marx (signature)

HARPO MARX

Jerry Mathers (signature)

JERRY MATHERS

Jackie Mason (signature)

JACKIE MASON

Marlee Matlin (signature)

MARLEE MATLIN

Tim Matheson (signature)

TIM MATHESON

Walter Matthau (signature)

WALTER MATTHAU

DEBI MAZAR

ALEX McARTHUR

JENNY McCARTHY

DOUG McCLURE

MAUREEN McCORMICK

JOEL McCREA

DYLAN McDERMOTT

DYLAN McDERMOTT (B)

RODDY McDOWALL (B)

RODDY McDOWALL

SPANKY McFARLAND

ELIZABETH McGOVERN

SHIRLEY MacLAINE

SHIRLEY MacLAINE (B)

KYLE McLAUGHLIN

DON McLEAN

RACHEL McLISH

ED McMAHON

STEVE McQUEEN

Best Wishes,
BUTTERFLY McQUEEN

JAYNE MEADOWS

AUDREY MEADOWS

COLM MEANEY

BILL MEDLEY

JOHN MELLENCAMP

SID MELTON

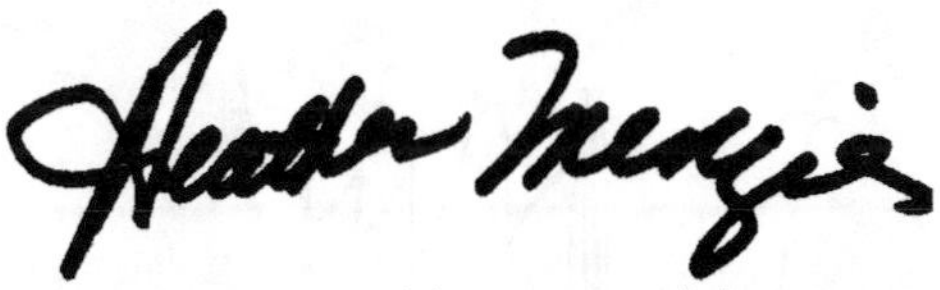

HEATHER MENZIES

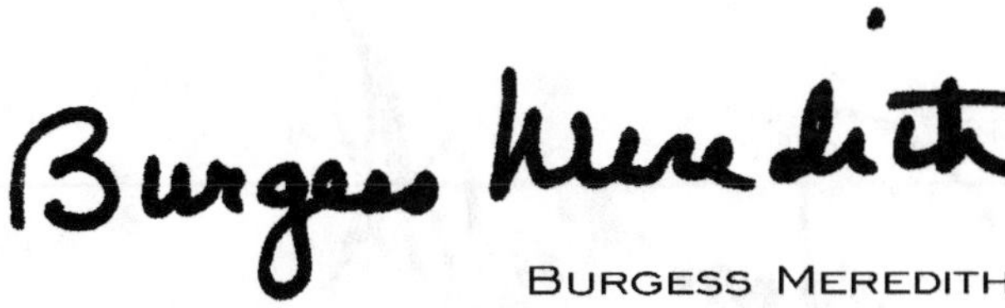

BURGESS MEREDITH

ALYSSA MILANO

VERA MILES

DENNIS MILLER

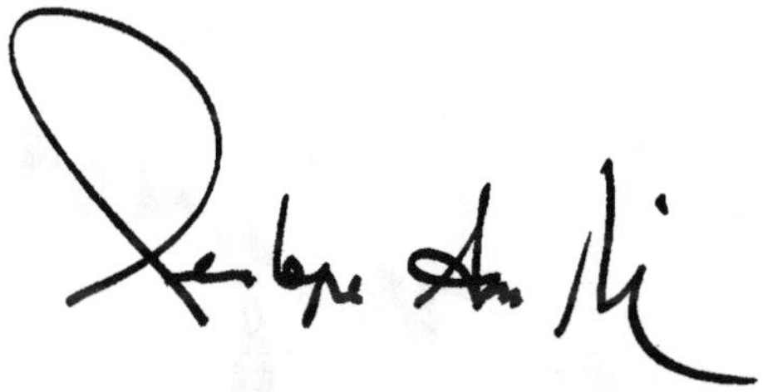

PENELOPE ANN MILLER

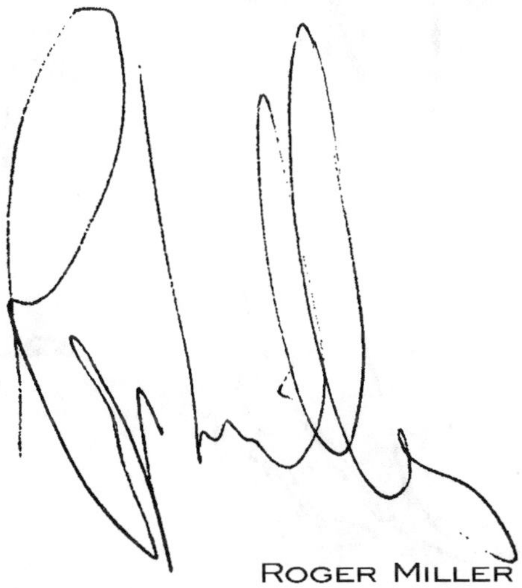

ROGER MILLER

ALLEY MILLS

DONNA MILLS

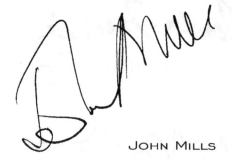

JOHN MILLS

JULIET MILLS

VINCENTE MINELLI

ANTHONY MINGHELLA

JAMES MITCHELL

WALTER MONDALE

MARILYN MONROE

RICARDO MONTALBAN

RICARDO MONTALBAN (B)

JOE MANTEGNA

BELINDA MONTGOMERY

DUDLEY MOORE

PEACE

DEMI MOORE

DEMI MOORE

MELBA MOORE

ROGER MOORE

ROGER MOORE (B)

PEGGY MORAN

RITA MORENO

ANITA MORRIS

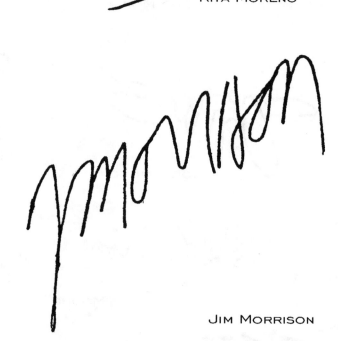

JIM MORRISON

ROBERT MORSE

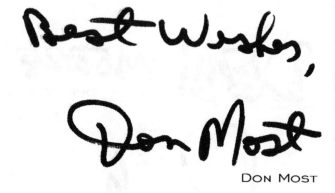

DON MOST

ARMIN MUELLER-STAHL

DERMOT MULRONEY

AUDIE MURPHY

EDDIE MURPHY

ANNE MURRAY

Best Wishes!

KEN MURRAY

MIKE MYERS

N

[signature]

JIM NABORS

[signature]

HARRIET NELSON

[signature]

CRAIG T. NELSON

All best wishes —
[signature] Mildred Natwick

MILDRED NATWICK

[signature]

JUDD NELSON

[signature]

RICKY NELSON

[signature]

JULIE NEWMAR

Enjoy!
Bob Newhart

BOB NEWHART

PAUL NEWMAN

"Patch"

HAING NGOR

STEPHEN NICHOLS

David Niven

DAVID NIVEN

GENA LEE NOLIN

RUDOLF NUREYEV

O

Mouseketeer
Cubby O'Brien

CUBBY O'BRIEN

HUGH O'BRIEN

MARGARET O'BRIEN

DONALD O'CONNOR

MAUREEN O'HARA

EDWARD J. OLMOS

TATUM O'NEAL

ANNETTE O'TOOLE

MAUREEN O'SULLIVAN

PARK OVERALL

P

AL PACINO

JANIS PAIGE

CHAZZ PALMENTERI

RAY PARKER, JR.

SARAH JESSICA PARKER

JACK PARR

JASON PATRICK

BUTCH PATRICK

Entertainment Edition

DENNIS PATRICK

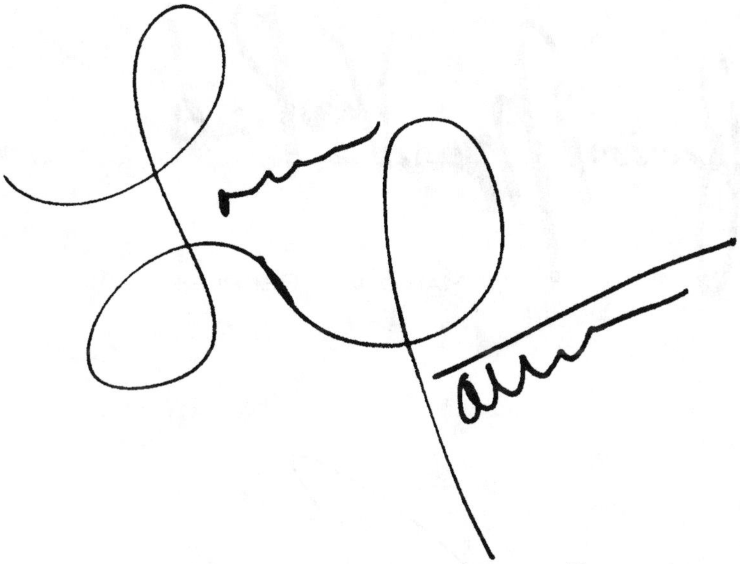

LORNA PATTERSON

PAT PAULSEN

BILL PAXTON

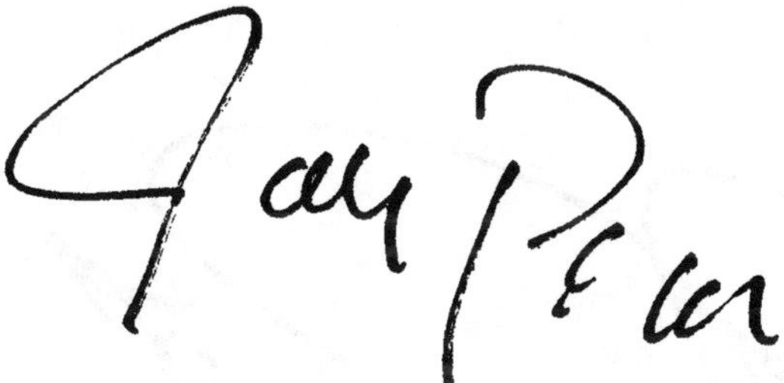

JOHN PAYER

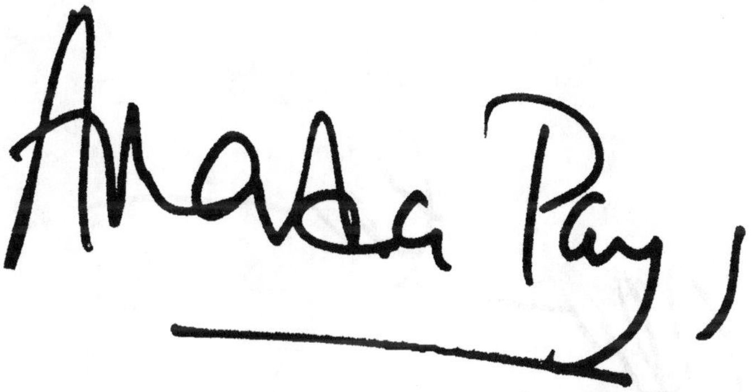

AMANDA PAYS

GREGORY PECK

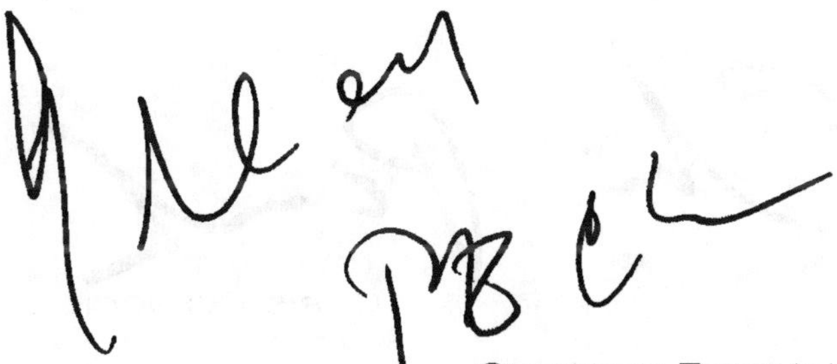

GREGORY PECK (B)

MARIO VAN PEEPLES

NIA PEEPLES

LISA PELIKAN

CLARA PELLER

CHRISTOPHER PENN

JANICE PENNINGTON

CHRIS PENNOCK

SEAN PENN

JOE PENNY

GEORGE PEPPARD

CARL PERKINS

MILLIE PERKINS

RHEA PERLMAN

RON PERLMAN

MATTHEW PERRY

MARIAH PERSCHY

JOE PESCI

WOLFGANG PETERSON

GARY PETTIS

TOM PETTY

REGIS PHILBIN

JULIANNE PHILLIPS

MICHELLE PHILLIPS

MACKENZIE PHILLIPS

RIVER PHOENIX

CINDY PICKETT

SLIM PICKENS

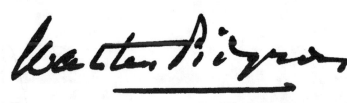

MARY PICKFORD

WALTER PIDGEON

CHARLES PIERCE

David Hyde Pierce (signature)

DAVID HYDE PIERCE

James H Pierce (signature)

JAMES PIERCE

Bronson Pinchot (signature)

BRONSON PINCHOT

Lou Pinella (signature)

LOU PINELLA

Danny Pintauro (signature)

DANNY PINTAURO

Joe Piscopo (signature)

JOE PISCOPO

Brad Pitt (signature)

BRAD PITT
(EARLY)

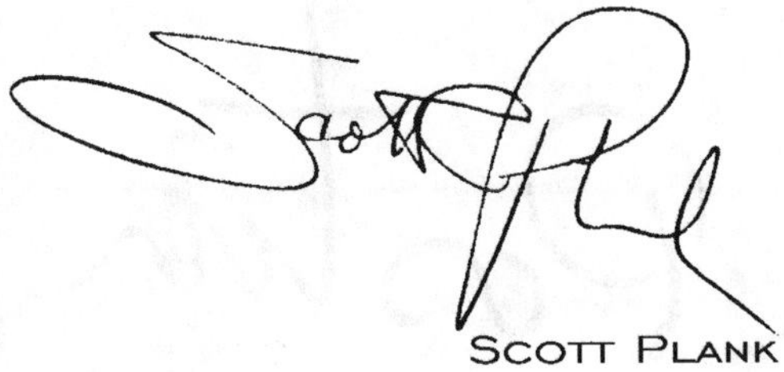

SCOTT PLANK

SUZANNE PLESHETTE

JOAN PLOWRIGHT

PRISCILLA POINTER

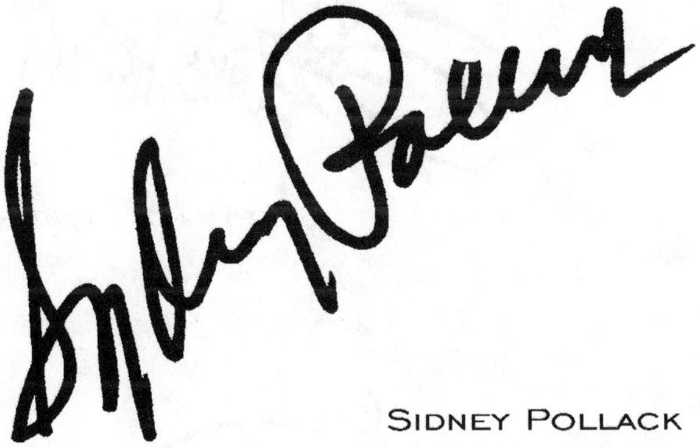

SIDNEY POLLACK

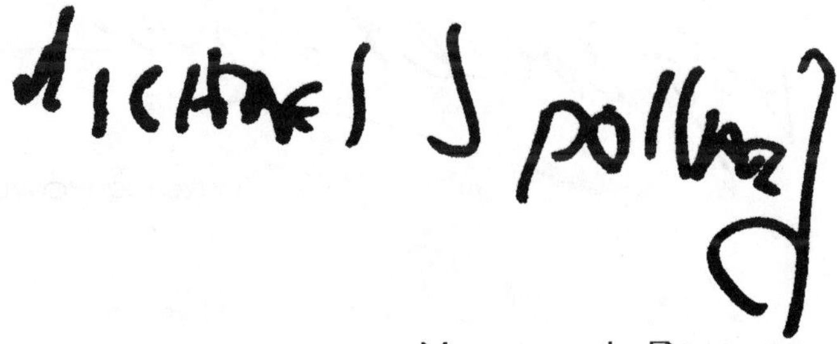

MICHAEL J. POLLARD

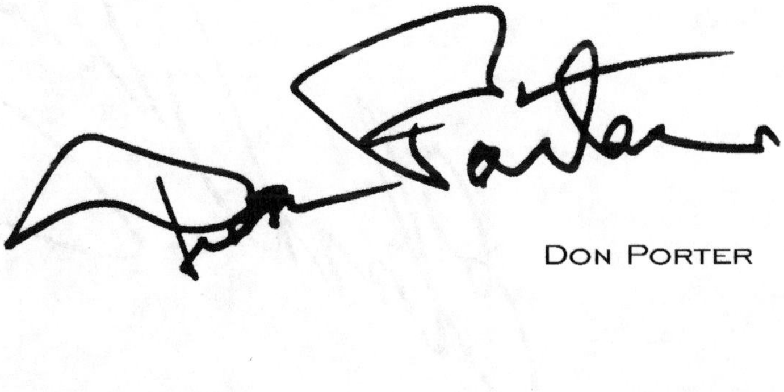

DON PORTER

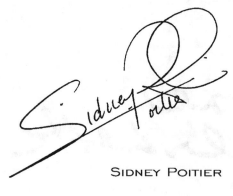

SIDNEY POITIER

TOM POSTON

ANNIE POTTS

STEPHANIE POWERS

TYRONE POWER

STEPHANIE POWERS(B)

ELVIS PRESLEY

PRISCILLA PRESLEY

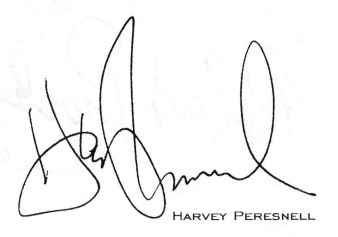

HARVEY PERESNELL

KELLY PRESTON

ROBERT PRESTON

VINCENT PRICE

CHARLEY PRIDE

FREDDIE PRINZE

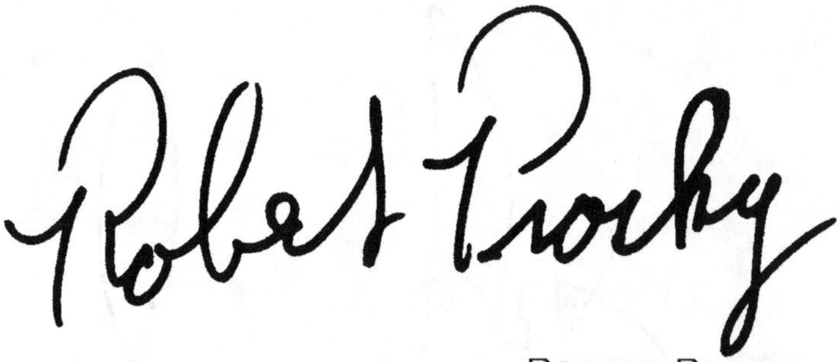

ROBERT PROSKY

JON PROVOST

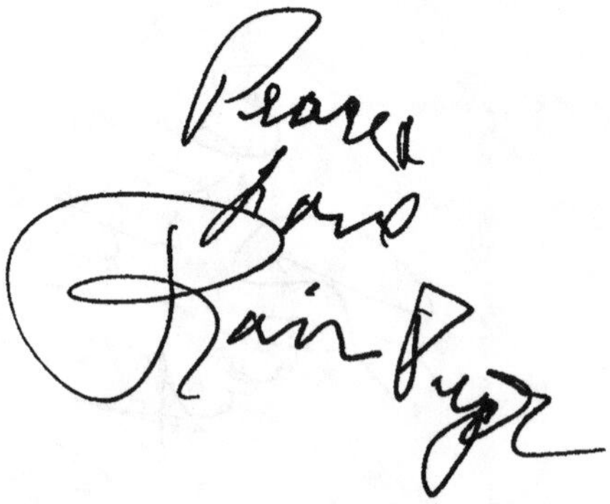

RAIN PRYOR

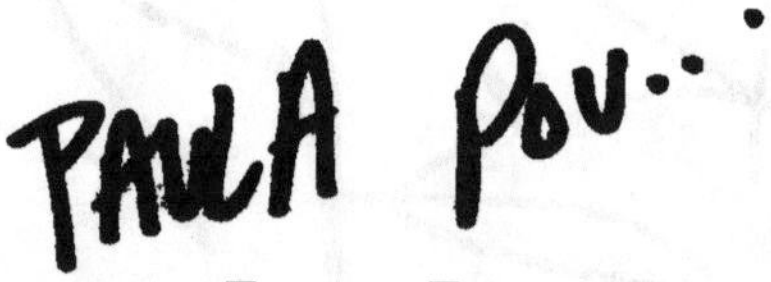

PAULA POUNDSTONE

DENVER PYLE

Q

RANDY QUAID

AIDAN QUINN

ANTHONY QUINN

ANTHONY QUINN(B)

R

My Best

George Raft (signature)

GEORGE RAFT

Love

Luise Rainer (signature)

LUISE RAINER

Claude Rains (signature)

CLAUDE RAINS

Ford Rainey (signature)

FORD RAINEY

Esther Ralston (signature)

ESTHER RALSTON

My Best

John Raitt (signature)

JOHN RAITT

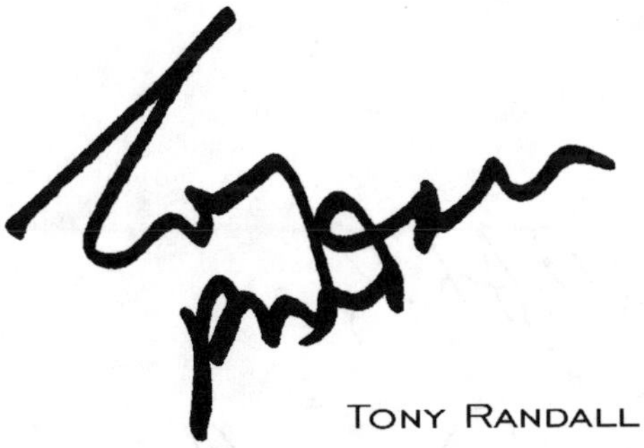

TONY RANDALL

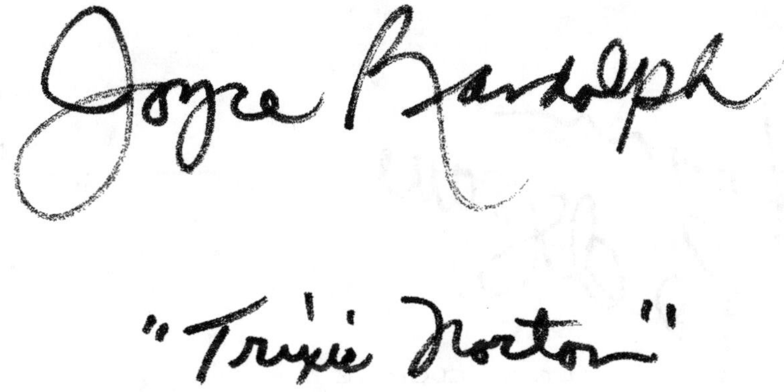

JOYCE RANDOLPH

"Trixie Norton"

JOYCE RANDOLPH

BASIL RATHBONE

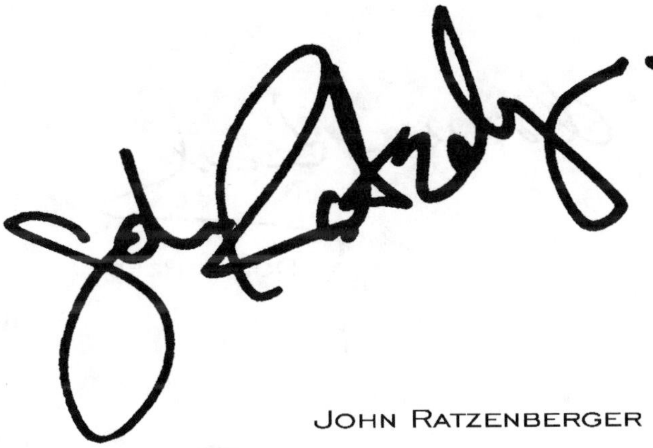

JOHN RATZENBERGER

LOU RAWLS

PAULA RAYMOND

RON REAGAN, JR.

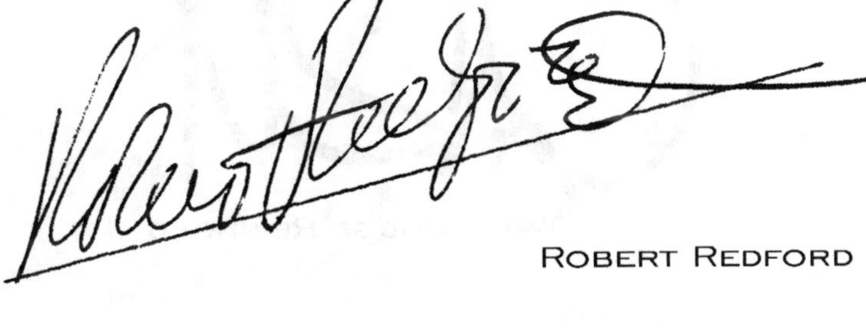

ROBERT REDFORD

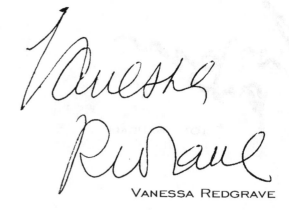

LYNN REDGRAVE

VANESSA REDGRAVE

DONNA REED

DELLA REESE

CARL REINER

ROB REINER

JUDGE REINHOLD

JEAN RENO

KELLY RENO

BURT REYNOLDS

DEBBIE REYNOLDS

JOHN RHYS-DAVIES

KEITH RICHARDS

KYLE RICHARDS

PATRICIA RICHARDSON

DON RICKLES

DIANA RIGG

LISA RINNA

GERALDO RIVERA

GERALDO RIVERA (B)

JOAN RIVERS

JOAN RIVERS (B)

HAL ROACH

JASON ROBARDS

JULIA ROBERTS

DALE ROBERTSON

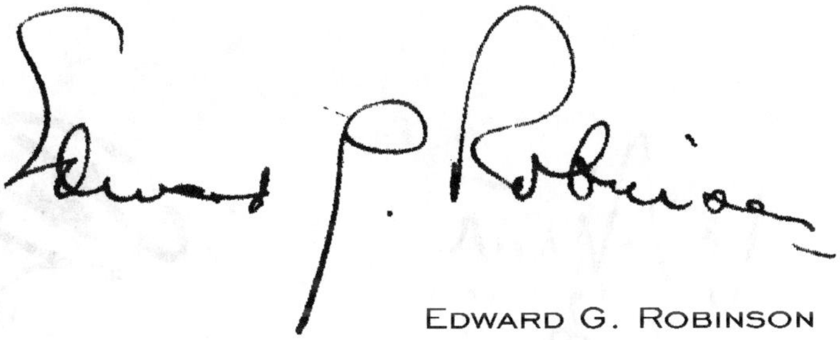

EDWARD G. ROBINSON

CHRIS ROCK

ROBERT ROCKWELL

GENE RODDENBERRY

BUDDY ROGERS

GINGER ROGERS

MIMI ROGERS

ROY ROGERS & DALE EVANS

WAYNE ROGERS

WILL ROGERS

GILBERT ROLAND

ESTHER ROLLE

CESAR ROMERO

JAMI ROSE

RU PAUL

MICKEY ROONEY

DAVID LEE ROTH

DAN ROWAN

GEOFFREY RUSH

HAROLD RUSSELL

Jane Russell

JANE RUSSELL

Ann Rutherford

ANN RUTHERFORD

Rene Russo

RENE RUSSO

Jeri Ryan

JERI RYAN

Peggy Ryan

PEGGY RYAN

Mark Ryder

MARK RYDER

ANTONIO SABATO, JR.

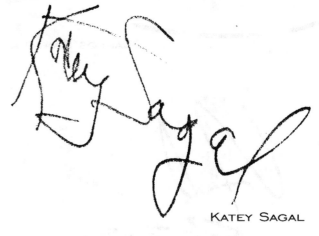

KATEY SAGAL

SOUPY SALES

PAUL SAND

JULIAN SANDS

ISABEL SANFORD

CARLOS SANTANA

CHRIS SARANDON

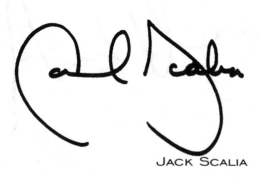

FRED SAVAGE

TELLY SAVALAS

JACK SCALIA

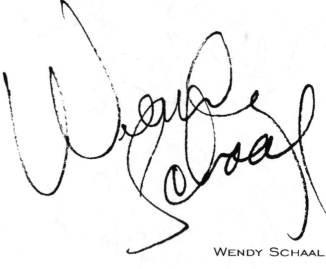

WENDY SCHAAL

CRAIG SCHAFFER

REBECCA SCHAEFFER

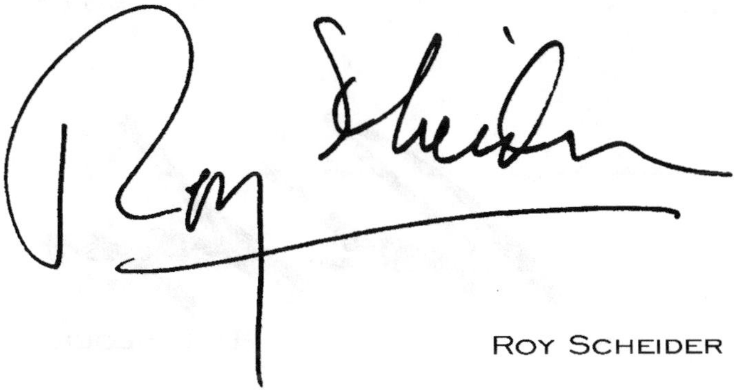

ROY SCHEIDER

DR. LAURA SCHLESSINGER

RICKY SCHROEDER (YOUNG)

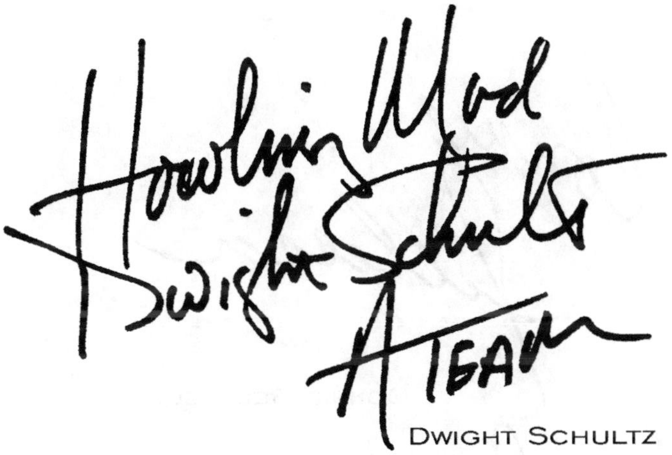

DWIGHT SCHULTZ

PAUL SCOFIELD

PETER SCOLARI

MARTIN SCORSESE

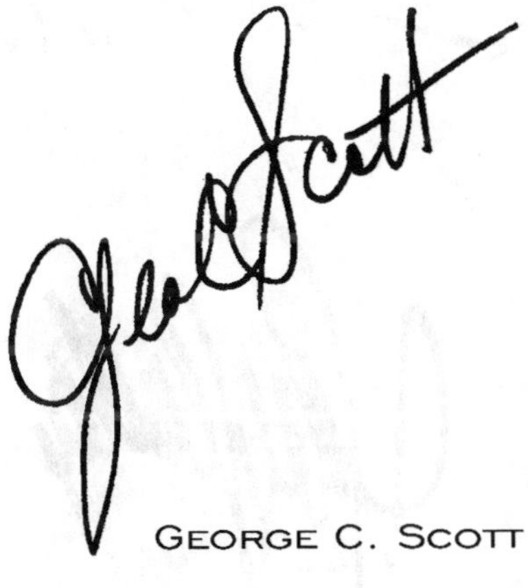

GEORGE C. SCOTT

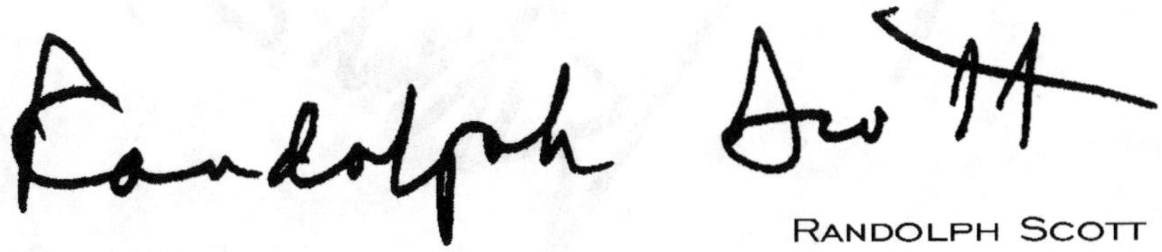

RANDOLPH SCOTT

STEVEN SEAGAL

BOB SEGER

CONNIE SELLECCA

TOM SELLECK

PETER SELLERS

JANE SEYMOUR

GARRY SHANDLING

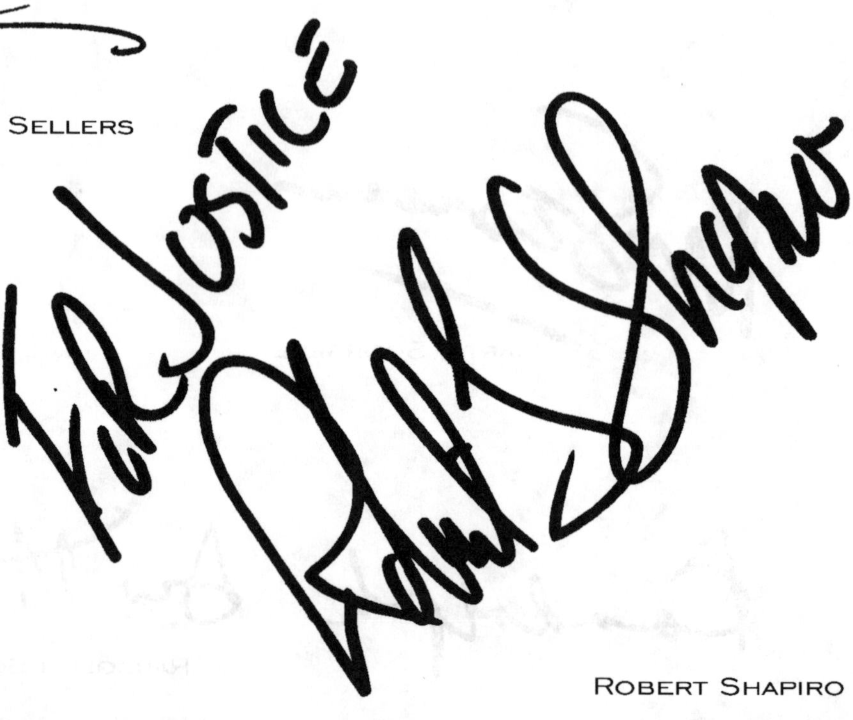

ROBERT SHAPIRO

ROBERT SHAW

NICOLLETTE SHERIDAN

PAULY SHORE

MARTIN SHORT

JOHN SCHUCK

ELISABETH SHUE

SYLVIA SIDNEY

ELIZABETH SHUE (B)

JONATHAN SILVERMAN

ALICIA SILVERSTONE

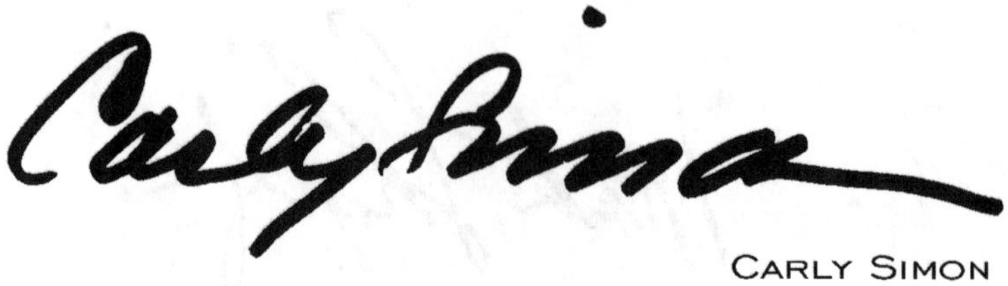

CARLY SIMON

FRANK SINATRA

SINBAD

LORI SINGER

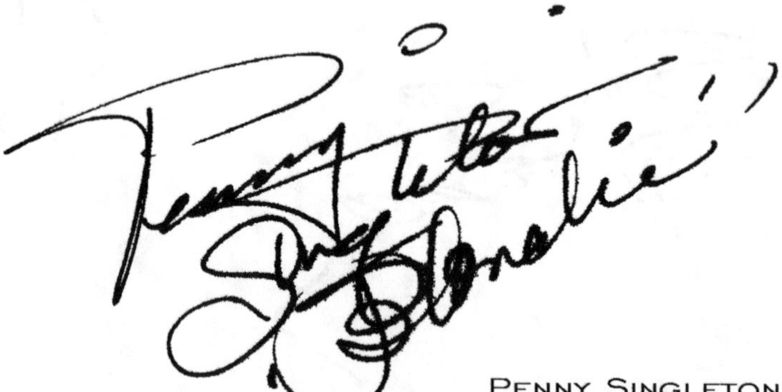

PENNY SINGLETON

GENE SISKEL

RED SKELTON

TOM SKERRITT

TOM SKERRITT (B)

MARK SLADE

CHRISTIAN SLATER

HELEN SLATER

ANNA NICOLE SMITH

MAGGIE SMITH

ROGER SMITH

JAN SMITH

JIMMY SMITS

REID SMITH

TOM SMOTHERS

WESLEY SNIPES

SUZANNE SOMERS

MIRA SORVINO

PAUL SORVINO

SISSY SPACEK

DAVID SPADE

JOE SPANO

DANA SPARKS

KEVIN SPACEY

TORI SPELLING

AARON SPELLING

WENDIE JO SPERBER

STEVEN SPIELBERG

SUSAN STAFFORD

FRANK STALLONE

SYLVESTER STALLONE

JOHN STAMOS

SYLVESTER STALLONE (B)

BARBARA STANWYCK

TERRENCE STAMP

JEAN STAPLETON

LEE STARKEY

Good Luck and
Best Wishes -
Kay Starr

KAY STARR

Good luck
from
Lili St. Cyr

LILI ST. CYR

MARY STEENBURGEN

ROD STEIGER

MARY STEENBURGEN (B)

DAVID STEINBERG

HOWARD STERN

CONNIE STEVENS

PARKER STEVENSON

With best wishes.

RISE STEVENS

SHAWN STEVENS

JAMES STEWART

JERMAINE STEWART

PEGGY STEWART

PATRICK STEWART

SUSAN ST.JAMES

SHARON STONE

love!
GALE STORM

(B)
SHARON STONE

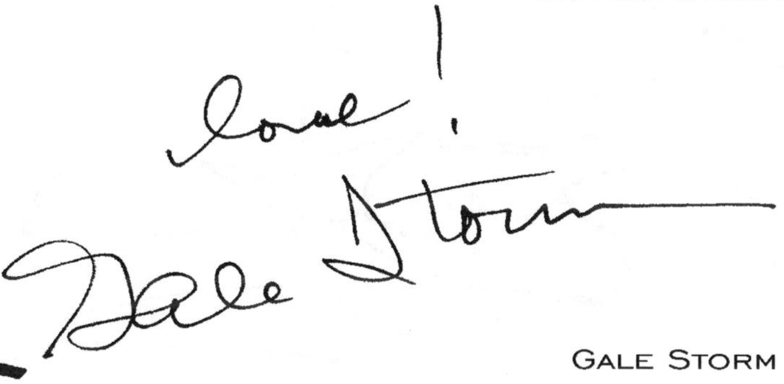

PETER STRAUSS

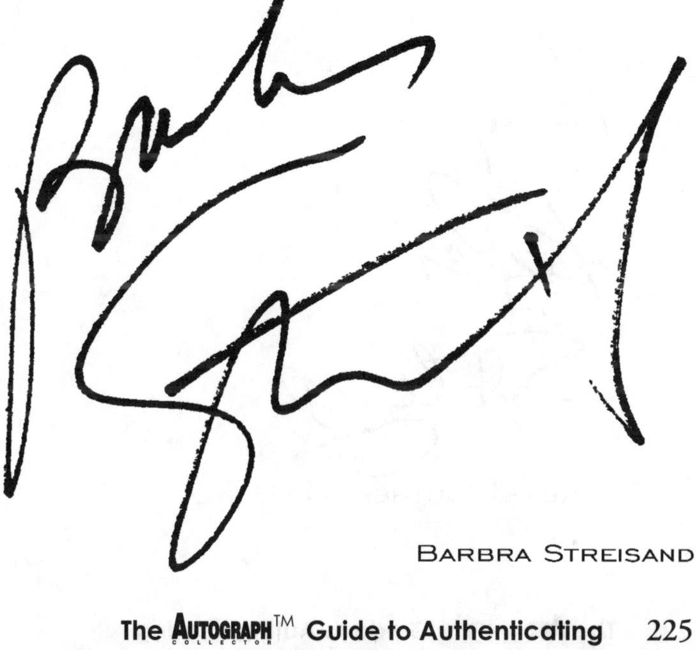

BARBRA STREISAND

WOODY STRODE

WOODY STRODE (B)

SUSAN SULLIVAN

YALE SUMMERS

DAVID SUSSKIND

DONALD SUTHERLAND

KEIFER SUTHERLAND

T

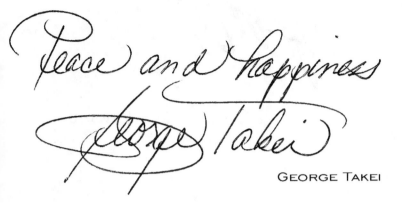

Peace and happiness

GEORGE TAKEI

JEFFREY TAMBOR

GLORIA TALBOT

LARENZ TATE

JESSICA TANDY

ELIZABETH TAYLOR

ELIZABETH TAYLOR
(B.)

LYLE TALBOT

JOSH TAYLOR

ROD TAYLOR

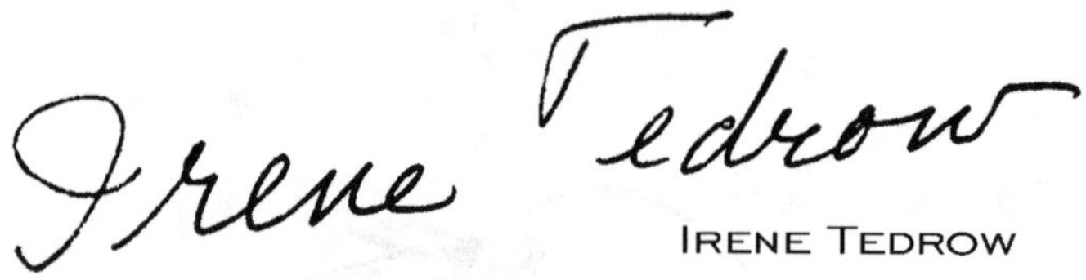

IRENE TEDROW

LAUREN TEWES

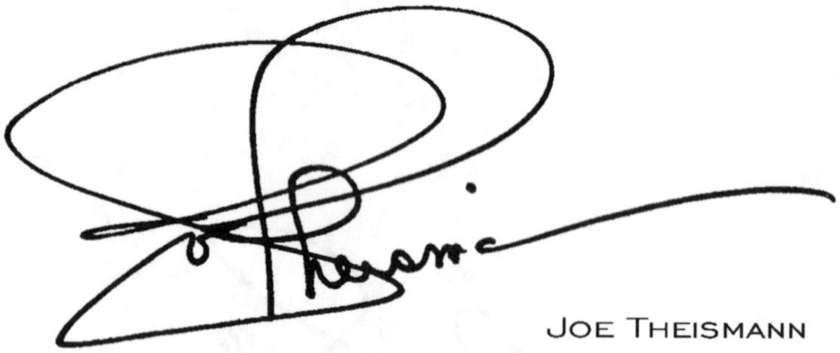

JOE THEISMANN

ALAN THICKE

BETTY THOMAS

ALAN THICKE (B)

DANNY THOMAS

HENRY THOMAS

HENRY THOMAS (B)

HEATHER THOMAS

JONATHAN TAYLOR THOMAS

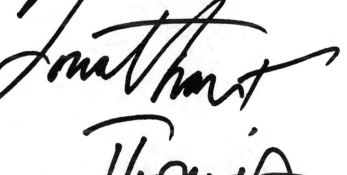

JONATHAN TAYLOR THOMAS (B)

MARLO THOMAS

MELODY THOMAS

LINDA THOMPSON

LEA THOMPSON

COURTNEY THORNE-SMITH

BILLY BOB THORNTON

BILLY BOB THORNTON
(B)

MOE   LARRY   CURLY

THREE STOOGES

CHERYL TIEGS

JENNIFER TILLY

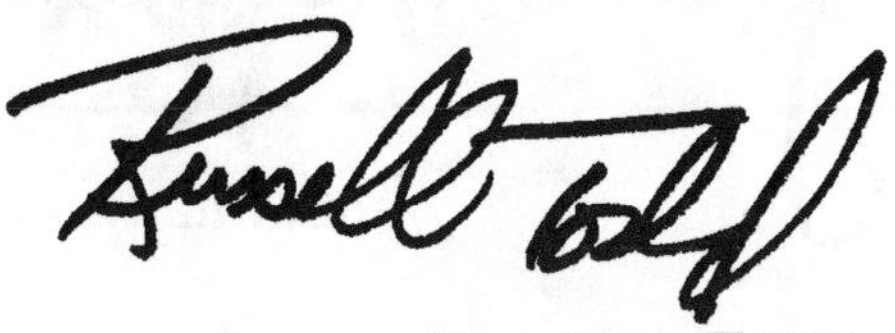

RUSSELL TODD

TAMLYN TOMITA

LILY TOMLIN

ANGEL TOMPKINS

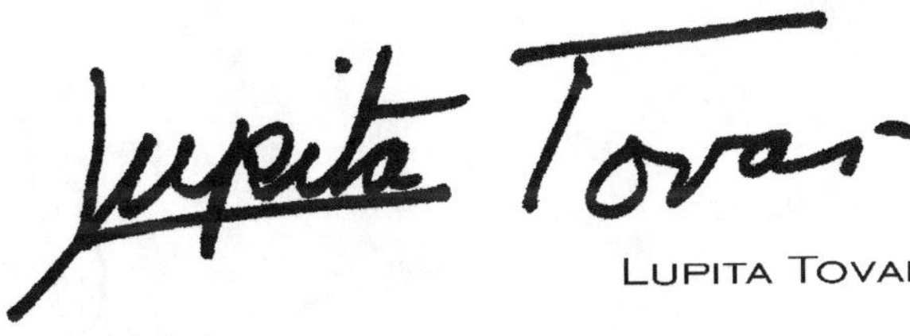

LUPITA TOVAR

SPENCER TRACY

JOHN TRAVOLTA

JEANNE TRIPPLEHORN

DONALD TRUMP

TANYA TUCKER

TOMMY TUNE

SHANNON TWEED

LIV TYLER

STEVEN TYLER

U

Tracey Ullman

TRACEY ULLMAN

Skeet Ulrich

SKEET ULRICH

Miyoshi Umeki

MIYOSHI UMEKI

Jay Underwood

JAY UNDERWOOD

V

Brenda Vaccaro signature

BRENDA VACCARO

Rudolph Valentino signature

RUDOLPH VALENTINO

Jean-Claude Van Damme signature

JEAN-CLAUDE VAN DAMME

MAMIE VAN DOREN

Eddie Van Halen signature

EDDIE VAN HALEN

Good Luck
Dick Van Patten
8

DICK VAN PATTON

Robert Vaughn signature

ROBERT VAUGHN

Robert Vaughn (B) signature

(B)

ROBERT VAUGHN

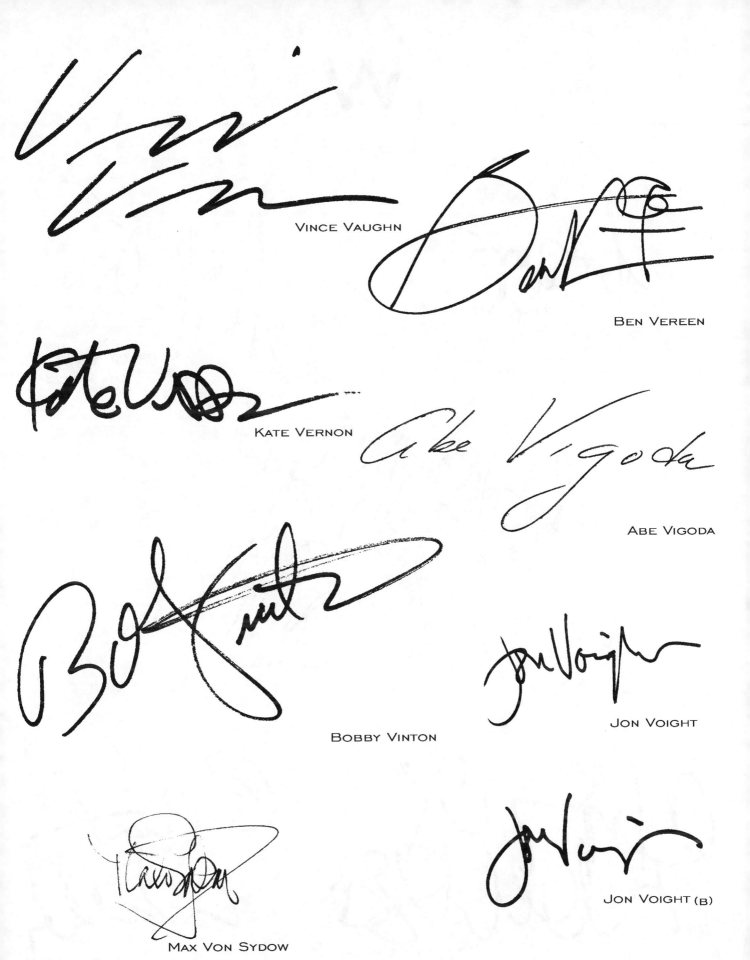

VINCE VAUGHN

BEN VEREEN

KATE VERNON

ABE VIGODA

BOBBY VINTON

JON VOIGHT

MAX VON SYDOW

JON VOIGHT (B)

W

LINDSAY WAGNER

LINDSAY WAGNER (B)

ROBERT WAGNER

CHRIS WALKER

CLINT WALKER

Always
Gr. Wall

GEORGE WALLACE

Best wishes
Eli Wallach

ELI WALLACH

Sherilyn Wolter

SHERILYN WOLTER

Sela Ward

SELA WARD

LESLEY ANN WARREN

DAVID WAYNE

JOHN WAYNE

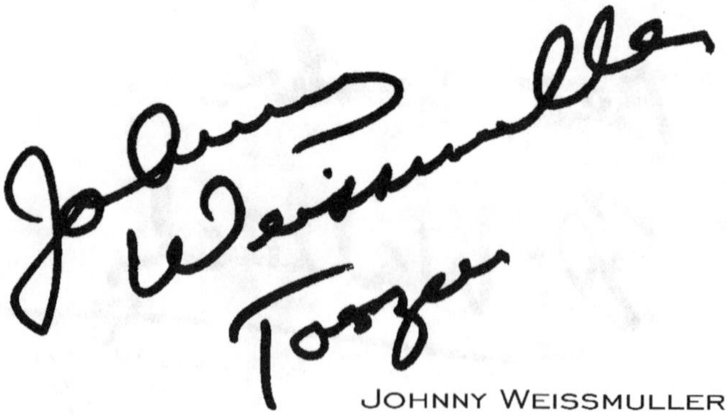

JOHNNY WEISSMULLER

RAQUEL WELCH

DAWN WELLS

ADAM WEST

DR. RUTH WESTHEIMER

JAMES WESTMORLAND

SHELLY WEST

MARK WAHLBERG

FOREST WHITAKER

Ian Whitcomb

IAN WHITCOMB

Best Wishes

Jesse White

JESSE WHITE

Vanna White

VANNA WHITE

Good luck!

Slim Whitman

SLIM WHITMAN

Shannon Wilcox

SHANNON WILCOX

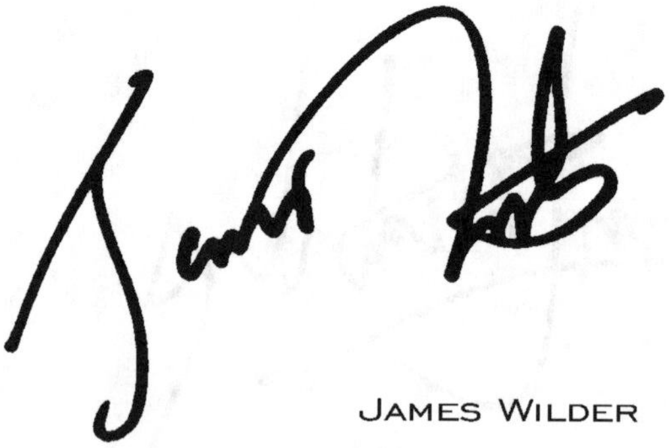

BILLY WILDER

JAMES WILDER

(B)
JAMES WILDER

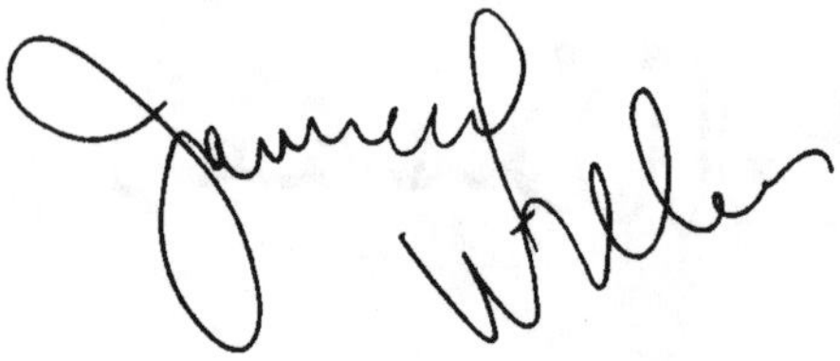

JAMAAL WILKES

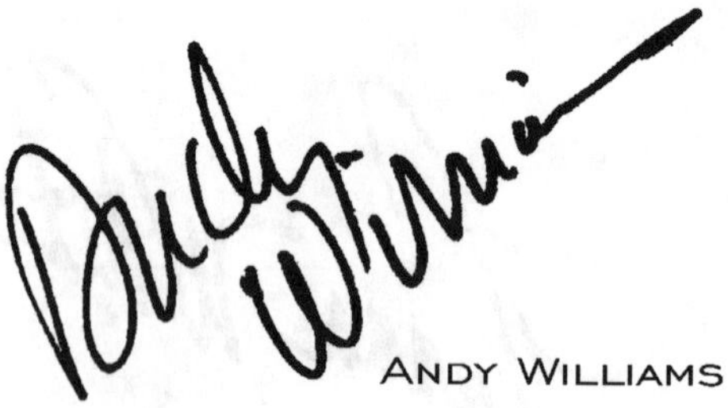

ANDY WILLIAMS

HANK WILLIAMS

JOHN WILLIAMS

ROBIN WILLIAMS

ROBIN WILLIAMS (B)

BRUCE WILLIS

BRIAN WILSON

JEFF WINCOTT

HENRY WINKLER

HENRY WINKLER
(B)

EDGAR WINTER

JONATHAN WINTERS

BILLY WIRTH

SCOTT WOLF

DAVID WOLPER

NATALIE WOOD

ALFRE WOODARD

JOANNE WOODWARD

SHEB WOOLEY

JAMES WORTHY

FAY WRAY

JENNY WRIGHT

FAY WRAY
(B)

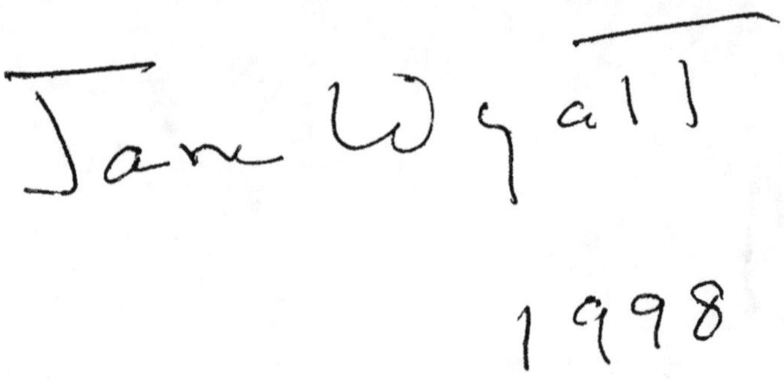

Jane Wyatt

1998

JANE WYATT

NOAH WYLE

JANE WYMAN

JANE WYMAN
(B)

MING NA WYNN

Entertainment Edition

"WEIRD AL" YANKOVIC

DWIGHT YOAKAM

LORETTA YOUNG

HENNY YOUNGMAN

NEIL YOUNG

ROLAND YOUNG

SEAN YOUNG

SEAN YOUNG (B)

VICTOR SEN YOUNG

Z

PIA ZADORA

GEOFF ZAHN

BILLY ZANE

STEPHANIE ZIMBALIST

DAPHNE ZUNIGA

AUTHORS

The following are authentic signatures of famous authors. Often they are less under siege from autograph collectors than movie stars. Why not try your hand at building a world class author collection?

JAMES LEE BURKE

GEORGE FRASER

TOM CLANCY

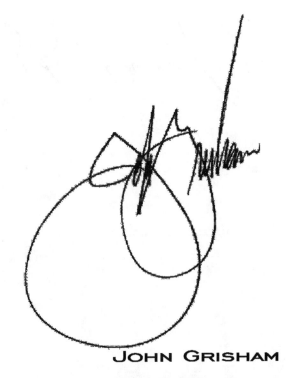

JOHN GRISHAM

MICHAEL CRICHTON

MICHAEL CRICHTON

STEPHEN KING

ANNE RICE

Boo!

DEAN KOONTZ

WIZARD OF OZ

Clara Blandick

CLARA BLANDICK
"AUNTIE EM"

Ray Bolger
The SCARECROW OF OZ

RAY BOLGER
"SCARECROW"

Billie Burke

BILLY BURKE
"GLINDA"

Jack Haley

JACK HALEY
"TIN MAN"

JUDY GARLAND
"DOROTHY" (1966)

JUDY GARLAND
"DOROTHY" (1939)

MARGARET HAMILTON
"WICKED WITCH OF THE WEST"

CHARLEY GRAPEWINE
"THE UNCLE"

CHARLEY GRAPEWINE
"THE UNCLE"

FRANK MORGAN
"WIZARD OF OZ"

BERT LAHR
"COWARDLY LION"

Collecting Tips:

The rarest of this cast are Clara Blandick and Charley Grapewine. Both were character actors who often went unrecognized by autograph hounds and died before Oz became popular in TV reruns after 1956.

Judy Garland is unaccountably scarce in signed Oz material, with signed photographs of her as Dorothy selling for as much as $4,000. Frank Morgan is equally rare on signed Oz pieces with a signed 8x10 as the Wizard selling for $9,000 at auction recently.

Hamilton, Haley, Bolger and many of the Munchkins can still be easily found by collectors.

GONE WITH THE WIND

Ward Bond [signature]

WARD BOND
"TOM, A YANKEE CAPTAIN"

Rand Brooks [signature]

"Charles Hamilton" [signature]

RAND BROOKS
"CHARLES HAMILTON"

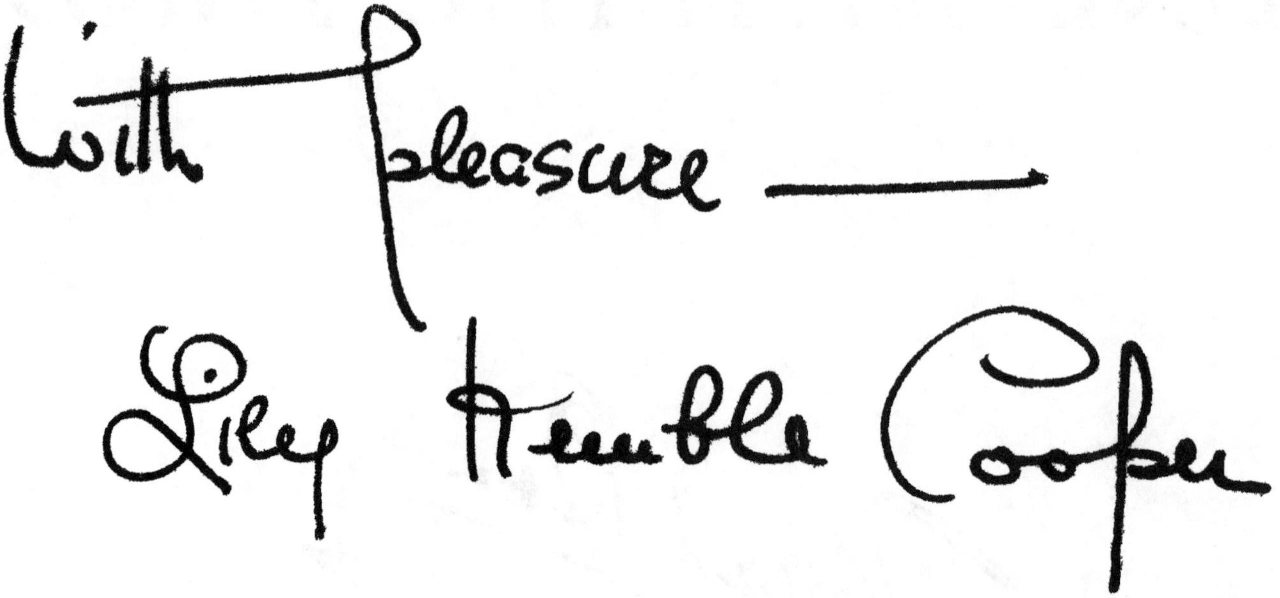

With pleasure —

Lily Kemble Cooper

LILLIAN KEMBLE COOPER
"BONNIE'S NURSE"

Fred Crane

FRED CRANE
"BRENT TARLETON"

Laura Hope Crews [signature]

LAURA HOPE CREWS
"AUNT PITTYPAT"

Jane Darwell [signature]

JANE DARWELL
"MRS. MERRIWETHER"

Sorry Best Wishes. Olivia 52 [signature]

OLIVIA DEHAVILLAND
"MELANIE HAMILTON"

Victor Fleming [signature]

VICTOR FLEMING
"DIRECTOR"

CLARK GABLE
"RHETT BUTLER"

LESLIE HOWARD
"ASHLEY WILKES"

VICTOR JORY
"JONAS WILKERSON"

EVELYN KEYES
"SUE ELLEN"

VIVIEN LEIGH
"SCARLETT O'HARA"

HATTIE McDANIEL
"MAMMY"

BUTTERFLY McQUEEN
"PRISSY"

THOMAS MITCHELL
"GERALD O'HARA"

ONA MUNSON
"BELLE WATLING"

CARROLL NYE
"FRANK KENNEDY"

BARBARA O'NEIL
"ELLEN O'HARA"

DAVID O. SELZNICK
"PRODUCER"

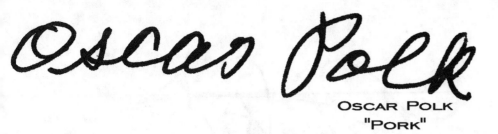

OSCAR POLK
"PORK"

GEORGE REEVES
"STUART TARLETON"

ALICIA RHETT
"INDIA WILKES"

EDDIE "ROCHESTER" ANDERSON
"UNCLE PETER"

ANN RUTHERFORD
"CAREEN"

Collecting Tips:

Butterfly McQueen is readily available on personal checks and often did sketches of - what else? A butterfly.

Vivien Leigh, while common in autographed material in general, is scarce on signed GWTW material.

Clark Gable and Hattie McDaniel are rare signed in character from the classic film.

GWTW is one of the most challenging casts to collect due to its large number of cast members.

SATURDAY NIGHT LIVE

More than 50 actors and actresses have starred as "not ready for prime time" players, making this an interesting collecting field.

JOHN BELUSHI

CHEVY CHASE

CHRIS FARLEY

BILL MURRAY

MIKE MYERS

LARAINE NEWMAN

GILDA RADNER

ADAM SANDLER

THEME IDEAS

In order to add both value and fun to your collection, try to keep a theme or some type of sanity to the madness of collecting! In the next few pages we give you a few ideas that might help you define your collection in the field of Entertainment, or at least get you started thinking of fresh and unique new ways to collect.

Get the Director of a film to sign along with a star or two! Often forgotten and less recognized on the street, directors are typically more valuable than many celebrities. This "ET" shot was signed by Steven Spielberg and child star Henry Thomas.

A few other directors who are willing signers are George Lucas, Tim Burton, Billy Wilder, Elia Kazan, David Lynch, Robert Altman and Ron Howard.

Voices carry, and are also interesting to collect. This famous cartoon parrot "Iago" from the Disney classic *"Alladin"* was voiced by comedian Gilbert Gottfried.

There are many famous voices still available for your collection: Thuri Ravenscroft (Tony the Tiger), Jean Vanderpyl (Wilma Flintstone), Mary Costa (Sleeping Beauty), Cammie King (Faline in Bambi), Charles Fleischer (Roger Rabbit) and Ilene Woods (Cinderella).

Cast photographs can be as simple and available as this one for the TV series *Lois & Clark* starring Dean Cain and Teri Hatcher, or as complicated to complete as M*A*S*H, Happy Days, or All in the Family. Challenging, but worth the wait.

People often complain that they can't find the photograph they like the best signed by their favorite star. In some cases, the particular photo you love may never have been signed and, if the star is deceased, .. never will be.

Solution? **Signature collecting.**

Find a nice example of your favorite celebrity's signature on a vintage album page or index card and then mat it with your favorite image.

Magazine signed covers are a popular collecting area. Below is a rare 1933 cover of a fan magazine signed in the period by Mae West, but some other popular collecting ideas include getting National Geographic, TV Guide, Time, Life and other magazines signed by the famous people who have graced their covers. We know of one collector who collects musicians signed on the covers of Rolling Stone, Billboard, Spin and other rock magazines. He now boasts a collection of over 500 signed covers and counting!

Cartoonists

Collecting original signed sketches by the legendary cartoonists of the world is fun and profitable. Although Bob Kane (Batman's creator) just passed away, his material is still readily available. Peanuts creator Charles Schulz is a must-have (he often signs simply Schulz), Matt Groening of Simpsons fame will usually sketch Bart for fans, and South Park Creators Matt Stone and Trey Parker will also sketch for fans. From Dilbert (Scott Adams) to The Family Circus (Bil Keane) and Dennis the Menace (Hank Ketchum) to Popeye (E.C. Segar) there are literally hundreds of cartoonists to collect from the past to the present.

In the Official Autograph Collector Price Guide (published yearly), all known collectable cartoonists are listed along with the current values of their sketches.

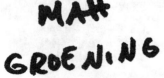

Collectors Tip:

A Charles M. Schulz full signature is usually older (more vintage) than a sketch signed simply Schulz. A full signature is worth slightly more than the last name alone.

Celebrity Sketches

One of the most unique collecting categories involves getting a celebrity to display their artistic skills by doing a sketch for you. Some stars like Vincent Price, Tony Curtis, Jack Lord and Red Skelton actually sold artwork professionally. Many stars try sketching themselves (self-caricatures) like George Takei, Vincent Price, Art Carney and Alfred Hitchcock.

DeForest Kelley draws a nice looking self-caricature, adding his most famous Star Trek quote for a fan.

Here is a rare sketch by Fred Gwynne of himself as TV's Herman Munster. Gwynne actually illustrated several childrens books in addition to acting.

James Stewart's famous Harvey sketches range in size from about 3x5 to 11x14 inches and are only going up in value since his passing.

Academy Award Collecting

One of the most popular collections to build is winners of the Best Actor and Best Actress Oscars from the first presentation to the present. Some collectors even try to collect the Best Directors, Composers and Best Supporting category winners. One collector told us he was building complete cast sets of signatures from each Best Picture winner.

SEAN CONNERY

GREER GARSON

WARNER BAXTER

GEORGE ARLISS

RICHARD BURTON

HUMPHREY BOGART

Rock & Roll Hall of Fame

Collecting all of the inductees in the prestigious Rock & Roll Hall of Fame is still within many collectors' budgets. The first inductees were inducted in 1986, and each year a handful of legends continue to fill out those hallowed halls. While it is true that many of these legends have passed on (making a trip to the bank and your favorite dealer necessary) many are still performing and signing for fans today.

Among them are artists Paul McCartney, Tina Turner, Gladys Knight, B.B. King, Jerry Lee Lewis, Johnny Cash and Elton John.

CARL PERKINS

JIM MORRISON

Sdrlennen
....
(J.W. Lennon)

Paul McCartney
....
(J.P. McCartney)

R. Starkey
....
(R. Starkey)

George Harrison
....
(G. Harrison)

THE BEATLES

*love
Gladys
Knight
1989*

GLADYS KNIGHT
Entertainment Edition

INDEX

APPENDIX

Recommended Periodicals

Autograph Collector
510-A So. Corona Mall
Corona, CA 91719
1-800-996-3977 or (909) 734-9636
1yr. subscription (12 issues) $38.00 US
www.AutographCollector.com

Pop Culture Collecting
510-A So. Corona Mall
Corona, CA 91719
1-800-996-3977 or (909) 734-9636
1yr. subscription (12 issues) $25.00 US
www.PopCulture.com

Recommended Books

The Official Autograph Collector Price Guide to Autographs   by Kevin Martin
The Standard in the field endorsed by the IACC & International Autograph Dealers Alliance
Over 60,000 values. Published Yearly $24.95 US
Odyssey Publication
In Bookstores Nationwide or call 1-800-996-3977 to order yours today

Signatures of the Stars   by Kevin Martin
An insiders guide to Celebrity Autographs $16.95 US
Antique Trader Publications
PO Box 1050 Dubuque, IA 52004
In stores Nationwide or call 1-888-689-7079 to order yours today.

Internet Auctions

www.AuctionUniverse.com
"The On-line auction you can trust"

www.Ebay.com
Over one million items in many categories including autographs.

Other Auctions and fine dealers can be found in the advertising section of this book.

Happy Collecting

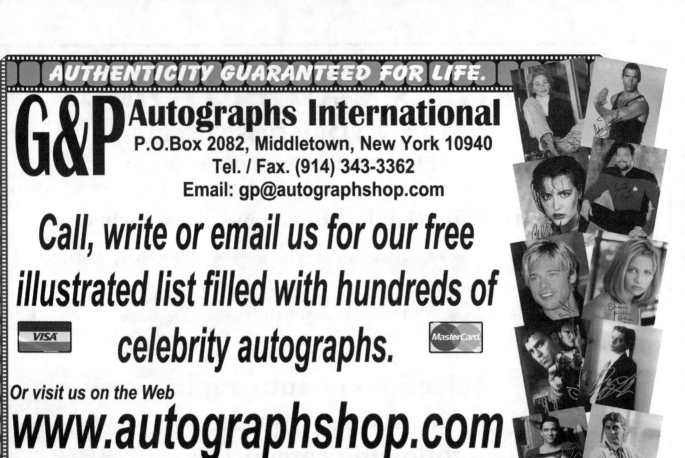

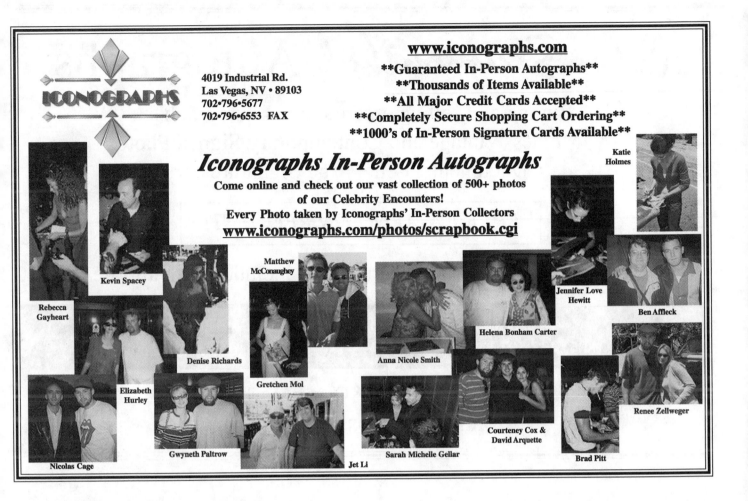

We offer a wide variety of material, in all fields, specializing in vintage Hollywood and historical figures. Our inventory is loaded with neat stuff!!

We also buy single items and collections. Call, write or e-mail with your offers. If you don't know what you have, ask anyway. It's a great hobby. We look forward to working with you.

Randy and Sharon Thern

IADA

Signatures In Time

P.O. Box 180
Scandinavia, Wis. 54977
Phone 715-445-3251 Fax 715-445-4691
E-Mail randy@signaturesintime.com or visit our web site at www.signaturesintime.com.

UACC

Member of UACC, IADA and Manuscript Society